GREEN PARADISE LOST

---

formerly WHY THE GREEN NIGGER?

ELIZABETH DODSON GRAY

ROUNDTABLE PRESS
WELLESLEY, MASSACHUSETTS

Grateful acknowledgement is made for permission to quote from the following:

Reprinted with permission of Macmillan Publishing Co., Inc. from *The Denial of Death,* by **Ernest Becker**. Copyright © 1973 The Free Press, A Division of Macmillan Publishing Co., Inc.

Eugene C. Bianchi and Rosemary R. Ruether, *From Machismo to Mutuality.* Copyright © 1976 by The Missionary Society of St. Paul the Apostle in the State of New York. Reprinted by permission of Paulist Press.

Glenn R. Bucher, ed., *Straight/White/Male.* Copyright © 1976 by Fortress Press. Reprinted by permission of Fortress Press.

Reprinted by special arrangement with Shambhala Publications, Inc., 1123 Spruce Street, Boulder, Colorado. From *The Tao of Physics* by **Fritjof Capra,** pp. 22, 23, 64, 66–69, 77–78, 141, 203, 244. Copyright © 1975 by Fritjof Capra.

Portions from *The Mermaid and the Minotaur* by **Dorothy Dinnerstein**. Copyright © 1976 by Dorothy Dinnerstein. By permission of Harper & Row, Publishers, Inc.

Erik Eckholm and Lester R. Brown, *Spreading Deserts: The Hand of Man.* Copyright © 1977 by Worldwatch Institute, Washington, D.C. By permission of Worldwatch Institute.

Portions from *The Male Machine,* by **Marc Feigen Fasteau**. Copyright © 1975 by Marc Feigen Fasteau. Used with permission of McGraw-Hill Book Company.

Portions from *The Male Attitude* by **Charles W. Ferguson**. Copyright © 1966 by Charles W. Ferguson. Reprinted by permission of Paul R. Reynolds, Inc., 12 East 412st Street, New York, NY 10017.

Ronald J. Glasser, M.D., *The Body Is the Hero.* Copyright © 1976 by Ronald J. Glasser, M.D. Used with permission of Random House, Inc.

From *A Sense of Seasons* and *The Shape of a Year* by **Jean Hersey**. Copyright © 1964 and 1967 Jean Hersey. By permission of McIntosh and Otis, Inc.

Portions from *Between Myth and Morning* by **Elizabeth Janeway**. Copyright © 1972, 1973, 1974 by Elizabeth Janeway. Used by permission of William Morrow & Co.

"Epiphany of Rain," by **Alexandra Johnson**. Reprinted by permission from The Christian Science Monitor. Copyright © 1976 The Christian Science Publishing Society. All rights reserved.

Portions from **Elisabeth Kuebler-Ross,** *Death: The Final Stage of Growth.* Copyright © 1975 by Elisabeth Kuebler-Ross. Reprinted by permission of the author.

Poems from *Green Winter* by **Elise Maclay**. Copyright © 1977 by Elise Maclay. Used with permission of McGraw-Hill Book Company.

"Beyond Words" by **Bunny McBride**. Reprinted by permission from The Christian Science Monitor. Copyright © 1977 The Christian Science Publishing Society. All rights reserved.

Excerpts from *The Love Letters of Phyllis McGinley* by **Phyllis McGinley**. Copyright © 1951, 1952, 1953, 1954 by Phyllis McGinley. Reprinted by permission of Viking Penguin Inc.

Excerpts from *Design with Nature* by **Ian L. McHarg**. Copyright © 1969 by Ian L. McHarg. Reprinted by permission of Doubleday & Company, Inc.

Used by permission of Charles Scribner's Sons from *Mind in the Waters* by **Joan McIntyre**. Copyright © 1974 Project Jonah.

What Do We Use for Lifeboats when the Ship Goes Down? by **My.** Copyright © 1976 by Observations from the Treadmill. Reprinted with permission of Harper & Row, Publishers, Inc.

Excerpts from *The Cosmic Connection* by **Carl Sagan,** produced by **Jerome Agel**. Copyright © 1973 by Carl Sagan and Jerome Agel. Reprinted by permission of Doubleday & Company, Inc.

Carl Sagan, *The Dragons of Eden: Speculations on the Evolution of Human Intelligence.* Copyright © 1977 by Carl Sagan. Reprinted by permission of Random House, Inc.

Material reprinted from *Plant Dreaming Deep* by **May Sarton,** with permission of W. W. Norton Co. and the author. Copyright © 1968 by May Sarton.

Reprinted, with permission, from *Should Trees Have Standing?* by **Christopher D. Stone**. Copyright © 1974 by William Kaufmann, Inc., One First Street, Los Altos, CA 94022. All rights reserved.

From *Mrs. Miniver,* by **Jan Struther**. Copyright © 1939 by Jan Struther; copyright renewed 1967 by J. A. Maxtone Graham. Reprinted by permission of Harcourt Brace Jovanovich, Inc.

Portions from *Lives of a Cell* by **Lewis Thomas**. Copyright © 1973 by the Massachusetts Medical Society. Reprinted by permission of Viking Penguin Inc.

Random lines of poetry from *Many Winters* by **Nancy Wood**. Text copyright © 1974 by Nancy Wood. Reprinted by permission of Doubleday & Company, Inc.

Library of Congress Catalog Card Number: 79–89193
ISBN 0-934512-02-8 (paperback); 0-934512-01-9 (cloth)

Contents

Part 1.
The Fall into Illusion

Part 2.
Whole and Home Again

Preface

An intellectual journey always has a beginning. It is possible the journey recorded in this book began in my earliest memory—a memory of golden sunshine and of being a child small enough to play sheltered among the massive white and blue hydrangea bushes in my yard. The sun is warm, and I feel contented and companioned by all that is around me. I think this is where my religious feelings first joined my feelings for nature. I have always felt connected in some profound way with the ultimate transcendent dimension of my life whenever I have allowed myself to experience the mystery and majesty of the created world.

I am grateful to my strong Southern Baptist religious heritage which fostered my connection to the transcendent dimension of life and also my perception of nature as the foundational communication of the Creator God. I am also grateful to my experience of motherhood which has powerfully motivated me to anticipate and care deeply about the time of my children and grandchildren on this planet.

A journey also has companions. I know it is not fashionable in today's feminist climate to say it, but many of my most significant companions on this intellectual and spiritual journey have been males.

Male writers usually have nurturing women, but women writers seldom have nurturing men to sustain them. My husband David has nurtured my body and spirit, affirmed my thinking, and constantly rejoiced in my selfhood as I have pursued these concerns. I have been fortunate to be part of this constantly stimulating and emotionally energizing colleagueship for the more than twenty-two years of our marriage. David edited this book, typed the final manuscript for me, designed the book itself, and finally used a word processor to typeset the book. I am grateful for his sharing my commitment and making this a "labor of love."

This book also would not have been written without the nurturing space provided by a four-year seminar about "Critical Choices for the Future," led by Carroll Wilson at the MIT Sloan School of Management. This seminar first introduced me to the limits-to-growth issues in late 1972. It was David who first suggested I join them. It was my friend Scott Paradise who first encouraged me to focus in my writing upon "the woman's perspective" I had found myself articulating in the seminar. And finally it was Carroll Wilson who had set the affirming atmosphere of the seminar, so that we all supported and encouraged one another as we explored "new think" about a sustainable future.

The stages by which first insights became a full-length book were nudged along at critical points by my dear friend Fontaine Belford. I had written my first major paper on the subject, "The Psycho-Sexual Roots of Our Ecological Crisis" in December 1974, and her affirmation that this was important thinking encouraged me to press on. I expanded that original paper for a project we were working on together—and it was she who challenged me to think and write about alternatives to the present view of things.

I have also been companioned for the last seven years by numbers of extraordinary women in the Theological Opportunities Program at Harvard Divinity School, whose depth of personhood in their mid-life blossoming gave me new insight and awareness of the different journey of a woman's life. Our students at Williams College, when we were visiting lecturers in the Environmental Studies Program during the fall of 1977, were most helpful in testing out various lines of thought. And I cannot forget my male as well as female colleagues in the U.S. Association for The Club of Rome. Their interest in and openness to these issues has led to continuing discussions in the Association about "The Masculine/Feminine Dimensions of the Global Problematique."

But finally it was the women's movement itself which provided the strong intellectual current which flowed through my head in the five years this book was gestating. I began my exploration of feminism in 1972 in a seminar at the Episcopal Theological School, "Women's Liberation and the Value of Human Being," taught by Olga Craven Huchingson. My graduate professional training in the early 1950s and my subsequent life in the ministry had led me to regard myself as already "liberated." I was not prepared for the perceptiveness of the emerging feminist analysis of patriarchy.

When my concerns in the limits-to-growth field led me to ask, *How did we ever think it was all right for us to do what we have done to nature?,* my readings in feminism and feminist theology began to suggest some tentative answers to that question. Valerie Saiving, Nancy Chodorow, Mary Daly, Rosemary Ruether, Elizabeth Janeway, and more recently Dorothy Dinnerstein—I am indebted to them all through their writings. They have helped me step back from some of the conventional assumptions of our culture to take a new look at our "mythology of reality."

Ultimately, the problem of patriarchy is conceptual. The problem which patriarchy poses for the human species is not simply that it oppresses women. Patriarchy has erroneously conceptualized and mythed "Man's place" in the universe and thus—by the illusion of dominion that it legitimates—it endangers the entire planet. This is the issue which in this book I am addressing.

My hope is that this book will help you join others in fashioning a better way of thinking and living for yourself and for those who come after you—a way that can be sustained and renewed not just for decades but for generations to come. I hope it will also leave you asking yourself: "What additional assumptions are there which are rooted in our male/female relationships and thus work quite unconsciously in our collective minds to undergird (and perhaps even conceal) what we are doing to ourselves, our world and our future?

Part 1.

The Fall into Illusion

This book has been a journey for me,
an intellectual and feeling journey.
It began on the seashore. I was looking out at the sea,
feeling powerfully in tune with the rhythms
of water and wave, wind and sun—
feeling at home in Eden.
I found myself asking:
How could we have done this to our Eden?
How could we have oppressed the natural world
  as we have?
How have we come to this perilous edge,
  a hair's breadth from losing our green paradise?
In this account of that journey
I will follow the path of the sea,
follow human footprints in the sands of time,
listen to the messages of the sea
and live with the moods of the sea.
Hang loose, then, to your images
and myths from the past.
Open up your intimations of new directions,
and come with me on this journey.

1.

Man-Above:
The Anthropocentric Illusion

We were walking along the beach yesterday and came upon an extensive walled city that had been constructed upon the sand in a marvelous way using driftwood and rocks and shells and sand. It was large and complex and intricate. Some unknown builders had labored long to construct it in the hours between high tide and low tide. But now the tide had turned and was coming back in upon that wondrous city in the sand, so that its hours were literally numbered. Our civilization is like that city in the sand. The tide has turned and time is running out for the way we have done things. But since the way we do is always based upon the way we think, what time is really running out on is our view of things, "the pictures about reality" which our culture has projected upon the cosmic walls of our universe.

God-Above and Man-Above

Walter Lippmann called them "the pictures in our minds of the world beyond our reach."[1] One such picture which has become deeply embedded in the lining of our minds is that of the Spirit God of the universe who is "above all and beyond all" and who created Man (Adam) to have dominion over all the animals and the rest of creation. Many theologians today remind us that "dominion" can mean responsible stewardship. But it is clear that—however "dominion" is interpreted—it always means "above" and implies a right to exercise power over others. In that centuries-old and mythically powerful story from the Book of Genesis in the Bible Man is conceived as definitely "above" the rest of nature. He partakes of the "spirit" character of the divine. He is created in the divine image. He gives all other animals their names, and so on.

This same consciousness of Man's place in the cosmic scheme of things is powerfully recapitulated in Psalm 8:3–8:

When I consider thy heavens, the work of thy fingers,
  the moon and the stars, which thou hast ordained;
what is man, that thou art mindful of him?
  and the son of man, that thou visitest him?

For thou hast made him little lower than the angels,
  and hast crowned him with glory and honour.
Thou madest him to have dominion over the works of thy hands;
  thou hast put all things under his feet,
all sheep and oxen,
  yea, and the beasts of the field,
the fowl of the air, and the fish of the sea,
  and whatsoever passeth through the paths of the seas.   (KJV)

The assumption here is that reality is indeed "Up-and-Down." We find God, imagined as "Pure Spirit," at the apex of a cosmological pyramid. Just below God come men (and I do mean males) created in the image of God by a specific act of God's creation (rather than being born of a woman as happens naturally). In this vision of things men are uniquely capable of communicating with God because of their unique spiritual nature.

Women and Nature Below

In this biblical view of the nature of things woman comes after and also below man. Woman was created (according to this chronologically earliest account of the Creation of the world in Gen. 2) out of man's body (rather than from a woman's body as happens naturally). She was created in order to be a function in man's life, to ease his loneliness, and to define her existence in relation to him by being a "helpmate" to him. Then come children, so derivative that they are not even in the Creation story. In this view children are obviously less "spiritual" in their formative years and thus suitable for being below. Then come animals, who do not have the unique human spirit at all—and thus while they live and move, they do not have "Being" as humans do. Thus animals are below. Further down still are plants, which do not even move about. Below them is the ground of nature itself—the hills and mountains, streams and valleys—which is the bottom of everything just as the heavens, the moon and the stars are close to God at the top of everything.

We need to distinguish here between what the biblical text actually said and how it has been interpreted by subsequent generations. There is in the first chapter of Genesis an account of the Creation written later than the Genesis 2 account. Like Psalm 8, it is

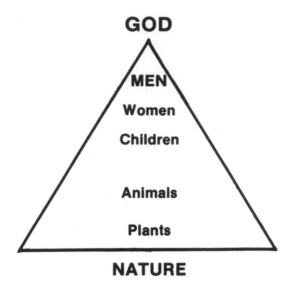

hierarchical and gives to humans dominion over all of nature, creating humans (male and female at the same time) in God's image. In the other account of the creation of the world written earlier (Gen. 2) the pattern might be described as anthropocentric rather than hierarchical—with everything created *around* the male, including the female created from his rib to be his helpmate.

However, the interpretation through the ages has blended the accounts in Gen. 1 and Gen. 2 into a single Creation Tradition, which has been both hierarchical and anthropocentric. While there is a distinction to be noted between what the Bible says and what generations of male theologians and preachers have understood the Bible to say, nonetheless the effect upon the lining of the cultural mind has come from these male interpretations, *not* from the biblical texts alone. The picture we have received is a product of Gen. 1 and 2 combined in a single tradition, and it was this combined Creation Tradition which provided us with our picture of the three-story universe of Heaven, Earth and Hell.

It should be no surprise to us that within that three-story view of the universe as it developed, the higher up you went, you approached heaven and all that is spiritual (i.e., invisible). In the opposite direction (down) you moved toward the devil, hell and the underworld of pain, punishment and torment—the place of all that centers upon what is fleshly, unspiritual, and by definition evil.

A Pyramid of Dominance and Status

I think we are a bit startled when we stand back and look at this hierarchical vision of reality. Expressed so baldly as I have just done, it gives us a bit of a shock. Yet we recognize that this pyramid of dominance and status embodies our accustomed sense that we live in a world in which some orders of being are by nature "above" others. From this hierarchical paradigm flow naturally such later philosophical distinctions (dualisms) as animate/inanimate, mind/body, spirit/flesh, transcendent/immanent, even culture/ nature and civilization/nature. Real "spirit"—the kind that is valued—dwells only in the top echelons of this pyramid. Lynn White in his famous article about "The Historical Roots of Our Ecologic Crisis"[2] correctly perceived that the pagan animistic view (which affirmed the presence of "spirit" in the lower realms of trees and rocks and streams) functioned to protect nature in a way that the pyramidal paradigm of the Judeo-Christian biblical world-view (which locates "spirit" only in the human and above) does not.

In the pyramidal paradigm even women, whom today we might view as equally human, are subordinate and inferior precisely on the ground of "spirit." It is rather shocking to us today to read some earlier Christian theologians on the subject of the kind of "spirit" present in women. Mary Daly cites St. Augustine's opinion that women aren't made in the image of God, and also St. Thomas Acquinas who defined women as misbegotten males.[3]

Women are now stepping back from these ancient religious myths, so basic to our Judeo-Christian and Western tradition. They are looking at these myths from the newly found perspective of a feminist consciousness and realizing that these myths are patriarchal—i.e., they rationalize and justify a society that puts men "up" and women "down."

But the creation myth also puts down children, animals, plants— and Nature itself. It is no accident that the Old Testament in the Book of Judges casually tells of a master's appeasing a crowd of drunken men who wanted his male guest by offering them instead his concubine—who was raped until she died.[4] The Book of Genesis tells how under similar circumstances Lot had offered a crowd of lustful men in Sodom his two daughters in order to protect his male guests.[5] It really is no accident then that this same Old Testment recalls with approval the patriarch Abraham almost sacrificing his son Isaac in order to test and strengthen his own faith and trust in God.[6] The right of the male is depicted as absolute over the life or death of females and children—whether for the male's convenience, for the protection of his male guests, or for the testing and strengthening of the male's religious faith.[7]

What is clearly articulated here is a hierarchical order of *being* in which the lower orders—whether female or child or animal or plant—can be treated, mistreated, violated, sold, sacrificed or killed at the convenience of the higher states of spiritual being found in males and in God. Nature, being not only at the bottom of this pyramid but being the most full of dirt, blood and such nasty natural surprises as earthquakes, floods and bad storms, is obviously a prize candidate for the most ruthless "mastering" of all.

Darwin's Vision

Another picture of the cosmos has been projected upon the cultural mind in the hundred years since Charles Darwin. This is a secular picture that lacks a divine Being. It is a picture in which Reality began at the bottom and at the beginning with a hot mass which over the centuries and millenia cooled and developed into the "primeval soup" from which came the compounds out of which all life slowly evolved through the ages, progressing slowly *up* the evolutionary ascent until we once again find Man at the top as "the most highly developed species."

Darwin's theory of evolution at first seemed to remind mankind that it was itself an outgrowth of nature over many ages (and not a product of a distinct act of creation by God as in the Genesis accounts). But finally even biological perspectives of evolution itself were interpreted to help man concentrate upon understanding himself as the most highly evolved species, with the most highly developed brain and consciousness—that for which the whole evolutionary process had taken place. What Darwin had visualized as *The Descent of Man* (2nd. edition, 1874)—suggesting that in our human family tree our forebears were animal species—came to be transformed in the popular mind into what J. Bronowski in his television series and subsequent book called *The Ascent of Man* (1973).

The similarity between these two pictures of cosmic reality is curious! Both assume quite unconsciously that Reality is hierarchical, having at its essence a grain, much as wood does, a grain that is profoundly "Up-and-Down" in character. Whether life is visualized as secular and evolving up from primeval compounds to the highly developed brain of Man, or whether life is visualized as religious and beginning with a top-down act of the divine who puts everyone and everything in its place, both views are equally and curiously clear that Man stands in a topmost position in the Up-and-Downness.

Up-and-Downness as "The Way It Really Is"

It is interesting in this context to contemplate the root meaning of the word "hierarchy," for it is derived from Greek words meaning "holy order." And certainly each of these cosmic visions has been viewed as a sanctified order, the one of them legitimated by religious authority and the other legitimated by a newer priesthood whose authority is scientific and academic and thus perceived today as qualified to tell us about "what is."

These two great cosmic visions of the order of things underlie the Western tradition and its great scientific and technological achievements. All of these achievements—from our splitting the atom to our walking on the moon, from our healing our diseases to the prolonging of our lives, from the multiplicity of new drugs, pesticides and laboratory-created compounds to the vastness of our industrial growth and productivity—all are predicated upon our confidence that Man is truly "above." They are predicated upon our confidence that his wants and needs and desires are the most important thing upon this earth. Underneath it all there is a confident assurance that what-is-above "calls the tune"—and that what-is-below will constantly be compliant and adapt. Hear that confident assurance in this comment by a professor at a great technological institution, speaking at a public meeting:

> The ancient Greeks trembled in awe before the piteous might of their tribal gods, but the thunderbolts Zeus had to throw around are nothing compared to the power science has put in the hands of modern man.[8]

Hear that assurance again in this comment of a graduate student at the same institution:

> I came here to build computers. The question is not how to appreciate the environment, but how to master it.[9]

Questioning the Divine Right of Kings

The power of science which is wielded with such confidence is born of the sense of himself which modern man has been given by the religious and evolutionary visions, namely, that he is indeed the most highly developed species with the best brain, one whose exploits must of necessity be "onward and upward." Man the thinker or Man the scientific researcher is not deterred even by the possibility of nuclear destruction or by the awesome hazards of DNA viral research.[10] Man's "right" to do these things is spoken of in terms reminiscent of earlier kings' defense of the divine right of kings. Surely this Man whose head is "crowned in flame" has, in this view, the right (if not always the wisdom) forever to blaze new trails, never to rest upon his laurels, always to think new thoughts, produce new miracles, prolong life, and, yes, create in the test tube new life itself. Whether blessed by God or by the evolutionary ascent, such a Man is only a little lower than the angels—and is justified in working to diminish even further that distance! Meanwhile all that which is below Man will stand in awe of his vast and varied accomplishments.

But wait. It doesn't seem to be working out that way. The ozone layer may be thinning, the pollution level thickening, the soil nutrients getting less and the water pollutants getting more. Species we have done away with, never thinking they'd be missed, it now appears "do" some things we did not know they did, which life needs done. How can this be? All these things—ozone, water, soil, lower species—all are "lower" than we. We have the illusion that their task is to provide us with what we want, to absorb our wastes, to get out of our way and not cause trouble. That is always what those "below" have been expected to do—women, children, Indians, Chicanos, blacks, so-called "primitive" peoples. They have always been overpowered by superior strength and "firepower." They have had to adjust and accommodate to that which was superior. How is it that now Nature will not do the same?

The answer comes back to us with the relentlessness of the tide we spoke of earlier: "It is because you are not right about who you are. Your city has been built upon the sands of an anthropocentric illusion. Castles built upon hierarchies which do not exist, simply cannot last."

2.

Does Human Uniqueness Mean Superiority?

The Jellyfish and Me

Pulling aside my curtains, I looked upon a clear and truly glorious day. The sky was a turquoise blue, without a cloud in its heavens. The sun was glistening on the fresh, cool water. Oh what a day to be alive! I jumped out of bed, quickly dressed, and drank a glass of juice. I was anxious to get outside and enjoy this beautiful summer day.

As I climbed over the rocks which connected us to the adjacent beach, I caught a glimpse of something glistening in the water below. I descended once again to the sandy shore to investigate. A large clear jellyfish, floating listlessly between here and the islands, had caught the sun's rays and thus appeared to me a reflector. My first reaction was that it was "*only* a jellyfish" and that I could not be bothered on a gorgeous day like today with something as miniscule and as unimportant of God's creations as a boneless, brainless jellyfish.

But that was just it! There are creatures like the jellyfish who are low on the evolutionary scale but are just as important and enjoy this beautiful day just as much as I do.

I realized, in these moments of identification with my fellow inhabitant, how anthropocentric my view of life had been. I realized how often I had gazed across the water and tried to envision all the humans on the other side, but how seldom I had tried to envision the other creations of God which inhabited the depths in between. This time as I climbed the rocks, I had a new appreciation of the world around me—the glorious day that was not just created for two-legged creatures like myself but for *all* creatures, even the floating jellyfish, to enjoy.[1]

My daughter wrote this for a college application. It was to be an essay on a memorable experience in her life, and she entitled it "Revelations on a Glorious Day." It particularly interested me because of its repentance of the anthropocentric illusion we have been discussing. People often ask me, "How could anyone honestly perceive that humans are *not* superior to the animals? We *are* smarter than they. We do have more highly developed brains. How can we *not* be 'higher' or 'superior'?"

9

Are Our Specialties So Extra-Special?

Our problem here is the great confusion in our thinking between our being "unique" as a species and our being "superior." Let me illustrate this confusion. A male friend once said to me in the course of a group's discussion of male/female, "But Liz, I *am* superior to you!" "Really?" I replied, "and how do you figure that?" "I am stronger than you," he said, "I can run a jackhammer and you can't." Another male present immediately testified that he couldn't run a jackhammer either, and did that make him inferior too? A female then pointed out that he could not bear a child and I could, so did that difference make *me* superior?"

This same confusion of thinking is to be found in our thinking about our relationship to animals. We always choose some attribute in which we humans happen to excel, and we then make that the basis for our conclusion that we as humans are not only different from other animals but also superior to them. For example, we sometimes choose arbitrarily to emphasize our more highly developed brain. But other animals have a more highly developed sense of smell or hearing or night vision. Why is any one particular attribute to be singled out as evidence of superiority as a species—except that we as humans always single out what we do best, just as men have done in asserting their superiority to women?

Why, for example, do we not recognize the dependence of all life upon the action of chlorophyll in green plants? All life—human, animal and plant—is ultimately dependent for its food-energy upon the photosynthetic process by which chlorophyll converts the sun's energy into food-energy usable by plants and by humans and other animals. Why do we not regard this as the most fantastic accomplishment ever, for all life in all its forms is derived from this? Or again, we are deeply dependent upon the phytoplankton in the ocean; we need the oxygen they put into the atmosphere. It is clear that we are deeply dependent upon them, while they can get along very well without any help from humans. How is it, we must ask once again, that we humans have come to think that our specialties are so extra special?

Now some would say that we humans are obviously "above" the other plant and animal species because we alone throughout history have been able to change the world so dramatically. We alone seem to have the power to eliminate other species, to bulldoze the face of the earth into new configurations, and to conquer time and space on our way to the moon and the planets. Surely, these people say, such exhibitions of human power and capacity prove our superior status as not only "unique" but also "above."

I would call this the king-of-the-forest syndrome. Would we say that a raging bull elephant is proving his "unique superiority" when he stomps the forest to pieces around him by his raw power to destroy? So too for us as humans. We clearly do have as part of our uniqueness as a species an obvious power to change (and destroy) the earth. But that uniqueness—dependent as it is for its basic sustenance in life upon other species and upon the biosphere—cannot therefore be construed as an absolute and unconditional superiority. What has happened is that once again, quite arbitrarily, we have decided upon one attribute—possessing powers such as our own—and said that these make us the superior species. Once again, we have declared that *what we do best* is the true measure of superiority.

Ranking by Brain Power: The Whales

But even if we consider just our most prized human possession, our brain power, we would do well to compare ourselves also with the whales and dolphins. If size alone determines the "brain hierarchy," then the dolphin easily ranks above both man and monkey.[2] But actually we think the most important thing is not the size of the brain but the development of the cerebral cortex. But even here the whales qualify. Peter Morgane, writing about his work on whales' brains and intelligence, says:

> The very fact that the whales have such a highly specialized nervous system makes them of immediate interest to man. It is almost mysterious to consider the meaning of the intricate fissurization... of the whale cerebral cortex. This is so vast and complex a neural territory that it has aroused considerable research interest in attempting to determine the significance of its complexity and regional specialization. Why are the cerebral hemispheres so large and luxuriantly folded? What is the explanation of all this exuberant cortex in animals that seem so restricted in their scope?[3]

The former director of the Cetacean (i.e., dolphin and whale) Brain Laboratory of the New York Aquarium, Myron Jacobs, has written that:

> The white whale...engages in complex play patterns which have their structural basis in this mammal's relatively large brain....Few mammals equal dolphins in their complex patterns of play, a behavior which seems related to large-brain mammals only.[4]

Peter Morgane has reflected upon man's characteristic expression of himself through the use of tools and our subsequent tendency to equate the use of such tools with intelligence. Is it not well, he suggests, to examine other possible modes of expressing intelligence or intellectual capacity?[5] Similarly, Carl Sagan has observed that "because whales and dolphins have no hands, tentacles, or other manipulative organs, their intelligence cannot be worked out in technology." Sagan asks:

> What is left? Payne has recorded examples of very long songs sung by the humpback whale; some of the songs were as long as half an hour or more. A few of them appear to be repeatable, virtually phoneme by phoneme; somewhat later the entire cycle of sounds comes out virtually identically once again.
>
> I calculate that the approximate number of bits of information (individual yes/no questions necessary to characterize the song) in a whale song of half an hour's length is between a million and a hundred million bits....Now, a million bits is approximately the number of bits in The Odyssey or the Icelandic Eddas.
>
> Is it possible that the intelligence of Cetaceans is channeled into the equivalent of epic poetry, history, and elaborate codes of social interaction? Are whales and dolphins like human Homers before the invention of writing, telling of great deeds done in years gone by in the depths and far reaches of the sea?[6]

Using then the standards of "brain power" which humans have established as their criteria for ranking animals, it is interesting that Man may not actually fill the topmost spot. Perhaps we have conquered the world because of our thumb—and not because of our brain. And perhaps our "social graces" are insufficiently developed for us to conquer the world without also destroying it.

By way of contrast with our human lack of "social graces" it is interesting to consider the cetologist Paul Spong's account of the social sense among orcas (the so-called "killer whales"):

> ...[W]e had gained our first glimpse of their exquisitely beautiful, efficiently and harmoniously organized existence.... We gained the impression that socially the population of more than fifty orcas was a cooperatively organized group entity comprising several pods which in turn subdivide in various ways; individual, pod, and population activities were obviously highly coordinated.[7]

Joan McIntyre has written in a similar vein about her observations of porpoises:

The porpoises will fish...for hours, long enough to satisfy their needs, but they do not quarrel about the fish. The sense of manners and propriety prevails, and once a porpoise is on a course for a fish, or has touched one, ownership is clear and undisputed.

The porpoises rarely fight with one another. The cohesion of the group does not allow the dislocation of arguments or grudges. Sometimes there is disagreement over a mate, and often a strange porpoise will be driven away from the school, but the order of the school itself is harmonious and, apparently, kind. There seems to be little reason to fight. There are no objects to accrue or own. There is constant sexual play, enough to allow everyone the satisfying contact with friends and mates and lovers. There is enough food. The school makes its way through the long hours, weeks, and years of its life with remarkable equanimity—and with great joy. Knit together by the integrated sensing of each member, each member sharing his or her information with the others, the school is an ancient, uniquely supportive culture—a creation greater than the sum of its parts.[8]

Three-Dimensional Communication among Dolphins

Language, symbolization, and communication are cited by some as what makes humans special. But here again we can understand only our human symbolization and we can only talk to other humans. Consider, on the other hand, the communication which is possible for the whale species. John Sutphen, writing about "Body State Communication among Cetaceans," has observed that:

In humans, communication is made largely through either verbal abstraction or visual imagery. The former is basically spoken and written language as we know it. Visual images, however, frequently transmit gestalt impressions and provide our most meaningful intra-species emotional link: the curl of the lip, the tear, the turn of the eyes. Vision, of course, is also our major stereotactic sense and serves functions of recognition and location. Imaging in the Cetacean world is primarily in the acoustic metaphor. Therein lies an incredible difference between human and Cetacean communication. Echolocation is three-dimensional. For example, one dolphin scanning another dolphin does not just receive an echo from the other's skin but from the interior body as well.[9]

Sutphen goes on to explore the implications for communication of the Cetacean capabilities:

Consider what exchanges of personal information may be possible between intelligent acoustic creatures. Each dolphin has to be constantly aware of the internal workings of the other if for no other reason than personal identification. From what is now known about the resolving capabilities of the dolphin's sonar and from certain well established principles of physiologic morphology of internal organs and tissues, it is reasonable to assume that Cetaceans are aware of each other's health and general well-being. Cancers and tumors must be self-evident. Strokes and heart attacks are as obvious as moles on our skins. Equally important, and perhaps more interesting, they could be constantly aware of a considerable portion of each other's emotional state. The psychophysiological alterations of sexual arousal, fear, depression, and excitement may be impossible to hide....To Cetaceans, then, there would be another order of magnitude of visualizable information, and another cultural experience to bring to bear on their meanings. What sort of candor might exist between individuals where feelings are instantly and constantly bared? It would be irrelevant to hide, to lie, or to deny one's feelings.[10]

That sort of mammal communication would involve a depth and sensitivity far beyond our human capacities. So extreme is the hearing-sensitivity of dolphins that they can hear a researcher drop a teaspoonful of water into a large oceanarium pool—and then echolocate the spot.[11]

"Mind in the Waters"

Those who work as researchers with the Cetaceans speak of their "awareness," and a book about Cetaceans is entitled *Mind in the Waters*. The editor of the book, Joan McIntyre, has written:

If you look for what might be the common thread in any number of stories about Cetaceans, you are struck with the recurring idea that it appears as if the animals are intensely conscious of what they are doing. Conscious in an exquisitely specific and finely detailed way. This business of being conscious of what you do may seem a simple one, but it is one we commonly do not grant to other animals. We tend to accept the idea that all animals other than humans behave like wind-up clocks of stimulus-response, that their lives are regulated only by instinct, and that the ability to be flexible, to react in a subtle changing way to changing circumstances, is an ability given only unto man—a kind of divine intercession....

But if we comb through our stories and our encounters with wild whales and dolphins, we find that they seem to hang together along a shining thread—that whales and dolphins know what they are doing, that their actions are purposeful, and stunningly specific to the occasion, that they intend us no harm, that they are *aware*.[12]

Malcolm Brenner describes his experience of such awareness, which came to him while he was trying to teach a dolphin named

Ruby to say her name in English, repeating it after him and rewarding her each time she improved by throwing her ball back to her:

> I threw the ball, and she returned it. "All right, now, say 'Ruby'! Rooo-beee!" Again that squawk. "No, you're going to have to do better than that.... C'mon, say 'Rooo-beee'!" For several more repetitions all I could get was that squawky noise. I noticed that *she was repeating the same sound every time;* it wasn't just any old squawk, but one with recognizable characteristics. But it was delphinese, which might as well be gibberish to me. I wanted English out of her, or at least a reasonable facsimile, and I was going to withhold the reward until I got it.
>
> Suddenly her vocalization changed. Her squawk came out in two distinct syllables, rather like the way I had been syllabificating "Rooo-beee!" I hurled the ball, and she returned it. Our progress became unbelievably rapid. In the space of five minutes, she began to copy the syllabification, rhythm, tone, and inflections of my pronunciation of the word "Ruby," and she did so with an accuracy and a speed I found amazing. Every time she came closer to my pronunciation I threw the ball, and she would return it to me. Each time her pronunciation was further away from mine I would withhold the ball until she improved. We became completely wrapped up in each other: the outside world ceased to exist. We stood a few feet apart in the water of her pen, staring at each other intently with bright eyes, and the excitement between us was palpable. Never in my life had I known such an intimate feeling of being in contact with an incredible non-human creature. It felt like it was what I had been created to do. Our minds seemed to running on the same wave. We were together....
>
> She repeated the word with this degree of accuracy a couple of times, then started babbling at me in delphinese, shaking her head up and down with her jaws open in that gesture, usually associated with pleasure, that I called "ya-ya-ing."
>
> I tried to get her to say "Rooo-beee!" again; more ya-ya-ing. Then she swam back a few feet and made a peculiar noise, a kind of "keee-orr-oop," but about three times faster than you pronounce it. It occurred to me—I don't know why—*to repeat that sound.* Ruby seemed to be expecting it of me. I did the best I could with it. She repeated it, but now it sounded slightly different; I mimicked her changes. God, she's doing to me what I was just doing to her! Where will this lead? By now the ball was forgotten; I was totally absorbed in listening to Ruby's vocalizations and was attempting to mimic them as accurately as possible with my inadequate human lips and vocal chords. She repeated the sound again, changed still more, and I copied that; she repeated it again, and as I tried to mimic her I thought, this sounds vaguely familiar—"kee-orr-oop." The light in my head went on. *The sound I had just successfully imitated was the one she had been giving to me in the beginning,* in response to my first attempts to make her say "Ruby!"

This realization struck me as the sound was coming out [of] my lips. Several fuses in my mind blew simultaneously and I did an incredible double-take, nearly falling over, and staring at Ruby, who was watching me with great concentration. When she saw the double-take, and knew I knew, *she* flipped out, and went ya-ya-ing around the pool, throwing water into the air, very excited, and apparently happy that this two-legged cousin of hers was progressing so rapidly. I just stood there, watching her, trying to figure out exactly what had just happened between myself and this dolphin.[13]

These researchers have come to know over time a number of whales, porpoises and dolphins, some in captivity and some free in the sea in groups. Many of the researchers speak of the conflict between our hierarchical understanding of these animals as "lower" and the "being" which they came to know as they interacted with them. In the opening words of *Mind in the Waters* Joan McIntyre writes:

We have, for too long now, accepted a view of non-human life which denies other creatures feelings, imagination, consciousness, and awareness. It seems that in our craze to justify our exploitation of all non-human life forms, we have stripped from them any attributes which could stay our hand. Try for a moment, if you can, to imagine the imagination of a whale, or the awareness of a dolphin. That we cannot make those leaps of vision is because we are bound to a cultural view which denies their possibility.[14]

John Lilly reported in connection with his early pioneering studies of dolphin behavior "a feeling of weirdness":

This effect was first noticed in our work in 1955, 1957, and 1958. As I became more convinced of the neuroanatomical size and complexity of the dolphin brain, I noticed a subtle change in my own attitude in regard to possible performances on the parts of these animals. To one like myself, trained in neurology, neurophysiology, and psychoanalysis, a large complex brain implies large complex capabilities and great mental sensitivity. Such capabilities and sensitivities can exist of course in forms we have not yet recognized....This opening of our minds was a subtle and yet a painful process....The feeling of weirdness came on us as the sounds of this small whale seemed more and more to be forming words in our own language. We felt we were in the presence of Something, or Someone, who was on the other side of a transparent barrier which up to this point we hadn't even seen. The dim outlines of a Someone began to appear. We began to look at this small whale's body with newly opened eyes and began to think in terms of its possible "mental processes," rather than in terms of the classical view of a conditionable, instinctually functioning "animal."[15]

Is the Problem Their Intelligence? or Our Communication?

I have lingered at such length with these various accounts of the whales, dolphins and porpoises because the researchers themselves became aware of the mental blinders which our hierarchical thinking and anthropocentric illusion had imposed. Joan McIntyre writes:

> Our perceptions, ideas, and feelings are filtered through the interpretative process of our culture; it is what we believe the world is about. It has, for several thousand years, insisted that we are unique and dominant in the world of life; that only we, the bearers of the technological literate tradition, learn; that to be this kind of human is to have as our dominion the materials of the planet to do with as we wish.

Citing the Genesis passage about God giving man dominion, she goes on to observe that "When we asserted our *rights* over nature we asserted our isolation and sanctioned a relationship that gives us not only the slaughter of whales for profit but also a belief system that could not imagine them as being like us."[16]

In a remarkably similar vein Carl Sagan writes in a book on the evolution of human intelligence about research on the intelligence of chimpanzees. Attempts to raise chimps with human babies had convinced many that chimps were incapable of abstract thought, because chimps did not learn to talk. But two psychologists, Beatrice and Robert Gardner at the University of Nevada, realized that the phrynx and larynx of the chimp are not suited for human speech. So they instead taught chimps Ameslan (American sign language, used by those unable to speak or hear). Ameslan was quite well suited to the great manual dexterity of the chimpanzee but has all the crucial design features of verbal languages. At the present time there are chimpanzees with working vocabularies of 100 to 200 words and using appropriate grammar and syntax. Washoe, Lucy and Lana have also used the sign language to invent new words:

> On seeing for the first time a duck land quacking in a pond, Washoe gestured "water bird," which is the same phrase used in English and other languages, but which Washoe invented for the occasion. Having never seen a spherical fruit other than an apple, but knowing the signs for the principal colors, Lana, upon spying a technician eating an orange, signed "orange apple." After tasting a watermelon, Lucy described it as "candy drink" or "drink fruit," which is

essentially the same word form as the English "water melon." But after she had burned her mouth on her first radish, Lucy forever after described them as "cry hurt food." A small doll placed unexpectedly in Washoe's cup elicited the response "Baby in my drink"....

Lucy was eventually able to distinguish clearly the meanings of the phrases "Roger tickle Lucy" and "Lucy tickle Roger," both of which activities she enjoyed with gusto. Likewise, Lana extrapolated from "Tim groom Lana" to "Lana groom Tim." Washoe was observed "reading a magazine"—i.e., slowly turning the pages, peering intently at the pictures and making, to no one in particular, an appropriate sign, such as "cat" when viewing a photograph of a tiger, and "drink" when examining a Vermouth advertisement. Having learned the sign "open" with a door, Washoe extended the concept to a briefcase. She also attempted to converse in Ameslan with the laboratory cat, who turned out to be the only illiterate in the facility. Having acquired this marvelous method of communication, Washoe may have been surprised that the cat was not also competent in Ameslan. And when one day Jane, Lucy's foster mother, left the laboratory, Lucy gazed after her and signed, "Cry me. Me cry."[17]

Finally Sagan tells a poignant story which raises clearly the question, Is our problem communicating with other species in their intelligence or in our communication?

Boyce Rensberger is a sensitive and gifted reporter for the *New York Times* whose parents could neither speak nor hear, although he is in both respects normal. His first language, however, was Ameslan. He had been abroad on a European assignment for the *Times* for some years. On his return to the United States, one of his first domestic duties was to look into the Garners' experiments with Washoe. After some little time with the chimpanzee, Rensberger reported, "Suddenly I realized I was conversing with a member of another species in my native tongue." The use of the word tongue is, of course, figurative: it is built deeply into the structure of the language (a word that also means "tongue"). In fact, Rensberger was conversing with a member of another species in his native "hand." And it is just this transition from tongue to hand that has permitted humans to regain the ability—lost, according to Josephus, since Eden—to communicate with the animals.[18]

The Eyeglasses of Culture through which We See

"We have the impression," Sagan writes, "that other animals are not very intelligent. But have we examined the possibility of animal intelligence carefully enough, or, as in Francois Truffaut's poignant film *The Wild Child,* do we simply equate the absence of our style of expression of intelligence with the absence of intelligence? In discussing communication with the animals, the French philosopher Montaigne remarked, 'The defect that hinders communication betwixt them and us, why may it not be on our part as well as theirs?' "[19]

Do you remember in *The Wizard of Oz* that everyone when they reached the Emerald City received green eyeglasses so that everything they saw looked emerald green? All of us have such eyeglasses. It is through these eyeglasses that we perceive our experience. These eyeglasses are the mental models or paradigms we use; as such, they constitute our culturally generated and shared basic interpretations of life.

These Cetacean and chimpanzee researchers experienced a basic "lens" (or paradigm or mental model) which we have all inherited as a cosmic vision. We use this lens in perceiving reality and interpreting its relationships and processes. When seen through this lens, reality is like a ladder or pyramid—"a great chain of being"—in which everything is either up or down, dominant or subordinate, superior or inferior, better or worse.

Seeing the "Different" as "The Other"

What I am saying is that when we are responding to *differences* (whether man and woman, or man and whale, or man and chimp, or man and God), our perceptions are dominated and distorted by the hierarchical paradigm. Almost in the same instant that we perceive difference, we are looking to ascertain rankings of power, moral or economic value, and aesthetic preference. We do this whether it is a different animal, a different culture, or a skin pigmentation that is different.

The hierarchical paradigm is thus not simply an ordinary eyeglass for our culture. It is a veritable contact lens. So intimately is it a part of how we perceive that we seem never to assess difference as just that—different. Instead we insist upon imposing comparative rankings which are incomplete and often self-serving.

Perhaps more important, we have in our Western tradition perceived what is different as "the Other." (This goes back to our hierarchical Judeo-Christian heritage and its perception of God as transcendent and thus Other.) And we have always set immediately to work ranking ourselves against that Other. If that Other is God, He is above me—superior. If that Other is female (and I am male), she is below me—inferior. If that other is animal, I am superior because I am more complex, more "highly developed," or because I am "created in the image and likeness of God." If that Other is another culture, it is probably below me because I do not understand it but at first glance it seems "more primitive," "less complex," or simply less powerful.

Legitimating the Power of Some over Others

Thus behind inequality, behind sexism, classism, racism—when these forms of social relationship and oppression are pursued back to their origins—you come finally to a common Gordian knot, which I have labeled *hierarchical thinking*. In its essence hierarchical thinking is *a perception of diversity which is so organized by a spatial metaphor (Up-and-Down) that greater value is always attributed to that which is higher.* This greater value which is attributed to that which is higher, legitimates the power of some over others—for, if you accept the Up-and-Down organization of perceptions and value which this metaphor provides, then inequality itself has been legitimated—when, in fact, prior to the metaphor of Up-Down one would have said only that there existed diversity.

It is ironic that many activist clergy, theologians and academics passionately concerned to fight oppressive systems, do not yet perceive how those same oppressions are rooted in and legitimated by the hierarchical thinking to which they still cling. "Why," some will ask, "is responsible stewardship over nature *not* an adequate safeguard?" Because so long as stewardship carries with it the illusion of superiority or *noblesse oblige* (as it now does), it is simply benign paternalism. *Power corrupts, and hierarchical categories legitimate that power.* I am amazed that many who are activists for social causes and who would never give the power of benign paternalism to slave owners, to government bureaucrats, or to corporate management, are strangely blind to the corrupting effects of that same sort of power inhering in benign paternalism when it is exercised over endangered animal species, the air, the waterways, the oceans, the soil, or "over" nature in general.

3.

Psycho-Sexual Roots
of Our Ecological Crisis

It is warm and the sun is hot on my body as I lie on the beach. I can feel the sun's warmth not only on my sunward surface but also where I touch the warm sand, which has been saving for me the heat of the day's sun. I am not too hot because the strong wind caresses my body as a lover would, up my arms and down my legs and over my breasts and face, continuously and constantly stroking my tiny surface hairs with freshness, with exhilaration, with movement.

The lapping of the water in a never-ending rhythmic melody caresses my ears, punctuated sporadically by the cries of the seagulls. My body and mind feel intimately connected as my body floods with total awareness of itself. I also feel connected to the rough warm sand, to the caressing wind, to the lapping water and the nearby gulls. I feel gloriously alive—and connected.

Severing Connections with "The Other"

Hierarchical paradigms and pyramidal views of the world would not have to concern us if they were not also powerful shapers of our attitudes toward nature, teaching us to hold at an emotional distance our experiences of being connected with nature.

The cosmic vision of a hierarchically ordered universe sets us off as "Other" than the earth. Yet the earth is our home, the animals are our travelling companions. We are certainly different from plants, but we are not apart; they are the original producers of all the food-energy we consume. We can see this severing of connections with "The Other" most clearly of all in the dissociation which takes place within ourselves as we cut ourselves off from full awareness and acceptance of our connectedness with the physicalness of our own bodies.

This severing is expressed in our Western tradition in the dualisms of mind/body and spirit/flesh which haunt so much of our theology, philosophy and even our psychology. Much of what has been thought and written in the West is an outgrowth of this hierarchical paradigm which places Nature "below." And from this belowness of Nature has followed the lowly status we assign to our human and mortal bodies, which so obviously participate in the change-processes of that denigrated Nature.

The Small God Who Nonetheless Will Die

Our Western tradition not only seeks to sever these connections; it poses for us a terrible question about our human meaning and identity, as Ernest Becker has pointed out in his Pulitzer Prize-winning book *The Denial of Death*. Becker lays out the development of psychology from Freud as well as existentialist thought from Kierkegaard on. Becker sees man confronting the existential paradox of his own life when he faces death. Becker writes:

> *We always knew that there was something peculiar about man, something deep down that characterized him and set him apart from the other animals. It was something that had to go right to his core,* something that made him suffer his peculiar fate, that made it impossible to escape. For ages, when philosophers talked about the core of man they referred to it as his "essence," something fixed in his nature, deep down, some special quality or substance. But nothing like it was ever found; man's peculiarity still remained a dilemma. The reason it was never found...was that there was no essence, that the essence of man is really his paradoxical nature, the fact that he is half animal and half symbolic.... *It was Kierkegaard who forcefully introduced the existential paradox into modern psychology, with his brilliant analysis of the Adam and Eve myth that had conveyed that paradox to the Western mind for all time....*

> We might call this existential paradox the condition of individuality within finitude. *Man has a symbolic identity that brings him sharply out of nature.* He is a symbolic self, a creature with a name, a life history. He is a creator with a mind that soars out to speculate about atoms and infinity, who can place himself imaginatively at a point in space and contemplate bemusedly his own planet. *This immense expansion, this dexterity, this ethereality, this self-consciousness gives to man literally the status of a small god in nature,* as the Renaissance thinkers knew.

> Yet, at the same time, as the Eastern sages also knew, man is a worm and food for worms. This is the paradox: he is out of nature and hopelessly in it; he is dual, up in the stars and yet housed in a heart-pumping, breath-gasping body that once belonged to a fish and still carries the gill-marks to prove it. *His body is a material fleshy casing*

that is alien to him in many ways—the strangest and most repugnant way being that it aches and bleeds and will decay and die. Man is literally split in two: he has an awareness of his own splendid uniqueness in that he *sticks out of nature with a towering majesty,* and yet he goes back into the ground a few feet in order blindly and dumbly to rot and disappear forever. It is a terrifying dilemma to be in and to have to live with.

The *lower* animals are, of course, spared this painful contradiction, as they lack a symbolic identity and the self-consciousness that goes with it. They merely act and move reflexively as they are driven by their instincts. If they pause at all, it is only a physical pause; inside they are anonymous, and even their faces have no name. They live in a world without time, pulsating, as it were in a state of dumb being. This is what has made it so simple to shoot down whole herds of buffalo or elephants. The animals don't know that death is happening, and continue grazing placidly while others drop alongside them. The knowledge of death is reflective and conceptual, and animals are spared it. They live and they disappear with the same thoughtlessness: a few minutes of fear, a few seconds of anguish, and it is over. But to live a whole lifetime with the fate of death haunting one's dreams and even the most sun-filled days—that's something else.[1] (Emphasis added.)

Here you have the whole ideology of hierarchy laid out in a single passage: *Man's uniqueness* which *"sticks out of nature with a towering majesty"; the aversion to and horror of the body; the "lower animals"* with their *"dumb being"* which gives us *our total freedom to kill them without a pang— while we humans cry for ourselves* because we *marvelous humans still participate in that awful mortality of the natural world.*

The Severing of "Nature's Values" from "Human Values"

In other passages Becker spells out further the dualisms implied by what he and others in the Western tradition now have seen to be the existential paradox of a "splendid uniqueness" that nonetheless "aches and bleeds and will decay and die":

Nature's values are bodily values, human values are mental values, and though they take the loftiest flights they are built upon excrement, impossible without it, always brought back to it.[2]

*   *   *

Animals are not moved by what they cannot react to. They live in a tiny world, a sliver of reality, one neurochemical program that keeps them walking behind their nose and shuts out everything else. But look at man, the impossible creature! Here nature seems to have thrown caution to the winds along with the programmed instincts. She [—note Becker's use of the female pronoun when referring to nature—] created an animal who has no defense against full perception of the external world, an animal completely open to experience.... He not only lives in this moment, but expands his inner self to yesterday, his curiosity to centuries ago, his fears to five billion years from now when the sun will cool, his hopes to an eternity from now.... *Man's body is a problem to him that has to be explained....* "This is one aspect of the basic human predicament, that we are simultaneously worms and gods" [Maslow]. There it is again: *gods with anuses.*[3] (Emphasis added.)

It is important to note here that Becker's horror of the body is *not* found in the Genesis myth, which looked upon the bodily creation of man and—unlike Becker—pronounced that it was good. Yet the extreme hierarchicalism of the biblical view has provided fertile soil for the growth of the mind/body split which is so pronounced in Becker. This body/mind split was taken up into the Christian tradition from the remnants of the Greek thought world which were still powerfully present in the Roman Empire in the early centuries of the Christian era. About these Greek antecedents Rosemary Ruether has written:

Greek culture developed the experience of body alienation and suppression in...philosophical terms. It regarded the true self as the soul or consciousness and saw the body as a demonic alien that must be suppressed in order to develop the integrity of the true self. This dualism of body and soul was read out into the dualism of male and female to symbolize women as the expression of the demonic agency of the sexual and the carnal that attacks and subverts the regnant mind or reason. Men identify themselves with the mind, women with dangerous carnality. This identification of women with the lower half of the body-soul dualism is especially developed in Aristotle, who divided humanity along the lines of this dualism into the "head people" and the "body people"; the dominators and the dominated. Males are by nature the "head people" who dominate; women are the "body people" who are by nature to be dominated.[4]

The Fear of Physicalness

As with the body, so too with sex. Sex is supposedly good in the biblical account, but has not been so interpreted throughout Christian history. Rosemary Ruether traces the development of this dualistic Greek tradition in Christendom.

This tradition was inherited by the Church Fathers who typically defined men and women along the lines of mind and body. But because they also saw the body as an evil and demonic principle and defined salvation as the suppression of bodily feelings, women came to be seen as special incarnations of evil or "carnality." The flight from the body and the world became specifically the flight from woman. . . .

It was out of this dual level of male-female symbolism that there developed the split image of the feminine in Christianity—the split between spiritual femininity, symbolized by the Virgin Mary and Christian virgins, and carnal femaleness, which is seen as the incarnation of the diabolic power of sensuality. This split continued to grow more and more intense during the Middle Ages until it erupted in a veritable orgy of paranoia in the late medieval period [1300s–1600s]. It can hardly be a coincidence that the same period that saw Mariology reach the greatest heights of theological definition and refinement with the triumph of the doctrine of the Immaculate Conception in nominalist theology also saw the outbreak of witch hunts that took the lives of upwards of one million women between the 14th and the 17th centuries.[5]

Becker goes further, and sex comes to be linked with the body and thus with death:

Sex is of the body, and the body is of death. As [Otto] Rank reminds us, this is the meaning of the Biblical account of the ending of paradise, when the discovery of sex brings death into the world. As in Greek mythology too, Eros and Thanatos are inseparable; death is the natural twin brother of sex.[6]

If this is the place of sex, what is the place of women in this extremely male-oriented view of life derived from Freud? You guessed it! It's bad news for women. Becker discusses the temptation of the genius to bypass normal human reproduction:

After all, anything that detracts from the free flight of one's spiritual talent must seem debasing. The woman is already a threat to the man in his physicalness; it is only a small step to bypass sexual intercourse with her; in that way one keeps one's carefully girded center from dispersing and being undermined by ambiguous meanings.[7]

Motherhood in Becker's view ties the woman to all that is dark and fearful about the body and nature:

The real threat of the mother comes to be connected with her *sheer physicalness*. Her genitals are used as a convenient focus for the child's obsession with the problem of physicalness. [It seems obvious that Becker here is taking a boy-child's viewpoint to be "the child's."]

If the mother is a goddess of light, she is also a witch of the dark. He sees her tie to the earth, her secret bodily processes that bind her to nature: the breast with its mysterious sticky milk, the menstrual odors and blood, the almost continual immersion of the productive mother in her corporeality, and not least—something the child is very sensitive to—the often neurotic and helpless character of this immersion. After the child gets hints about the mother's having babies, sees them being nursed, gets a good look at the toiletful of menstrual blood that seems to leave the witch quite intact and unconcerned, there is no question about her immersion in stark body-meanings and body-fallibilities. The mother must exude determinism, and the child expresses his horror at his complete dependency on what is physically vulnerable. And so we understand not only the boy's preference for masculinity but also the girl's "penis-envy." [Note the shift, verbalized, to the viewpoint of a girl-child.] Both boys and girls succumb to the desire to flee the sex represented by the mother; they need little coaxing to identify with the father and his world. He seems more neutral physically, more cleanly powerful, less immersed in body determinisms; he seems more "symbolically free," represents the vast world outside of the home, the social world with its organized triumph over nature, the very escape from contingency that the child seeks.[8] (Emphasis added.)

The Deeply-Felt Roots of Our Culture's View of Nature

We owe Ernest Becker a debt of gratitude. The way we think and feel about nature has roots which are both intellectual and psycho-sexual. Distorted though I feel Becker's world view is, the widespread acclaim his book has received in literary and academic circles suggests that the view of our Western heritage he presents is not his alone.

Becker illustrates with marvelous clarity the point I wish to make: *Our culture's view of nature is deeply embedded not only in a hierarchical view of reality but also in deeply-felt attitudes toward what it views as the bearers of sheer physicalness, namely, sex, women, mother, and death.* I will explore in the next two chapters how these attitudes toward nature and physicalness came to be so deeply rooted in the male psyche.

4.

From Nature-As-Mother to Nature-As-Wife

It seemed pitch-black to me as I stepped out of the lighted room onto the darkened porch facing the water. I could make out nothing in the blackness at first. But as I paused, I could hear the lovely sounds of the shore at night—the rain falling vigorously on the deck beside me, the slurp-slosh of the tide as it lapped its way around the cove, the gentle sad sound of the gulls calling, the quiet throb of an approaching tug hauling a barge of trap rock down to New York City.

Off to my right I could see the lights of boats moored by the dock shimmering in long streaks from them to me. Slowly, from beyond the rocks on my left, came the tug lit with white lights like a Christmas tree and moving with dignified solemnity down the channel.

Then gradually, as I stood and listened to these gentle beach sounds, I began to be able to distinguish visual patterns. The railings and stairs to beach level. The straight mast of the sailboat I knew was pulled up on the beach. The chairs and tables on the porch. Even the shape of our black cat as she prowled the deck beside me.

The damp smell of the sea and the rain breathed around me as I sat and listened and watched. Slowly the tug grew smaller and smaller and finally disappeared into the distance. But the tide and the rain and the gulls and the shimmering streaks of dock lights stayed in a constant moist fabric of companionship with me. I could shut it all out by going back inside and closing the door, but while I lingered to prolong the evening, we were in dialogue.

Have people always felt this immediacy of their natural environment, I wondered?

I felt wrapped around, pervaded, "wombed" by the shapes and sounds and moist smells of the sea environment—as pervasive and immediate an environment as that cast out by the television medium, which equally reaches out to enfold us. I was a participant, who received the visual images, took in the smells, registered the sounds on sensitive eardrums. And my breathing added to the moist air even as it unconsciously synchronized its rhythm with the regularity of the waves.

How could we humans get so out of step to these rhythms?...so out of dialogue with these receptions?...so out of participation in this immediacy?

Culture as Male

The thinking and writing of history, philosophy, theology, and literature through the ages have been almost exclusively a male enterprise. Cultures world-wide have been dominated in their life by the decisions and thought-world of males. What difference has this made?

Charles Ferguson has addressed this question in his historical study, *The Male Attitude.*

Men have kept the records of the race.

They have decided what to tell and how to tell it, the impressions to leave and how deeply those impressions are to be engraved. First with the chisel, then with the stylus, then with the pen, then with the speeded keyboard of the typewriter and the beneficence of the printing press, men have multiplied words into elaborate systems of thought,*and the spine and ganglia of all these systems are male presumptions.* Men have associated and identified the acceptable with the masculine. They have given their opinions the name of philosophy and theology. They have sung the songs and the sagas, wrought the dramas and the operas. They have drawn and painted the pictures, seeing what the male saw and sees. *They have made the estimates and appraisals and served as the sole critics of what men have done en masse.*[1] (Emphasis added.)

*   *   *

Enjoying exclusive custody of language in written form, the scribe was quite naturally unaware of himself as male when it came to recording his deeds and his views. Clothes of the late Middle Ages were designed and cut to emphasize a man's equipment. Ostentatious codpieces called attention to his genitals. In writing, however, there was no need to display his structure or to connect it with his writing. Rather he could present his views as personal and individual opinions or proudly as eternal verities handed down through him.[2] (Emphasis added.)

*   *   *

Men presented the way they acted as if it followed the natural course of events, sometimes deplorable but in the main inevitable. I could not find in my reading cases where men watched themselves, even out of the corner of their eyes, behave as males. It was always I. Men might cry out as individuals ("I am the master of my fate, the captain of my soul") or they might evolve prodigious theories of human behavior and designate them as natural laws and *these might express an obvious and unmistakable masculine bent, but men seemed wholly unaware of the sex origin of their ideas.*[3] (Emphasis added.)

*   *   *

The male thinks of himself as the universal, so that you find much about Man (embracing Woman) in such stentorian terms as Man's Unconquerable Spirit, Man and His Destiny, Man and Civilization, Man and His Gods, Man Above Humanity, Man and the Future, Man Against Nature, Man and the Universe.

All of these terms, appearing in titles or subtitles, represent idealized concepts and have nothing to do with sex. *They project gender to its ultimate. And it is projected also into the infinite,* for the very idea of the Very God is expressed commonly, not to say solely, in the masculine. To refer to God as feminine gets a laugh from shock or embarrassment. *The godhead is encased by theologians, virtually all of them men, in phrases that preserve and sanctify the male ego.*[4] (Emphasis added.)

Charles Ferguson has documented in his extensive historical study the rise of what he calls "the male attitude" in the Western tradition, particularly during the past five hundred years. Those reassured by academic respectability might like to know that the eminent Yale historian C. Vann Woodward "read the manuscript as a friend and criticized it as a historian." What, then, does Charles Ferguson's work signify for our earlier consideration of "the pictures in our minds of the world beyond our reach"? Certainly we must take a closer look at the picture of the cosmic pyramid or hierarchy; and we must ask if this Up-and-Down metaphor has roots not just in the human psyche but in the male psyche.

The Maleness of the Genesis Myth of Creation

For example, let us examine the Genesis creation myth for clues to its sexual origin and sexual perspective. We begin by noting that the Genesis myth reverses the "normal" processes of birth—so that man is not born of woman but woman is born from the body of man. She is not only created second, but as an afterthought and in response to male need and is intended to fit around his life. Rather than his body being made from the life processes of a woman's body, she is made from his body. Charles Ferguson suggests that the male relationship to the machine provides the appropriate backdrop against which to view the Genesis myth:

> Emotionally, the dream of the machine is very old, and a kind of reverence for it can be spotted in some early sacred writings when the machine process was equated with the performance of the Deity or with deities. In the Hebrew account of Creation, the Deity is represented as Maker. He turned out the heavens and the earth in six working days. He made the world, the whole wide world, in a six-day week, and threw in man for good measure, using such raw materials as were at hand, and then He went on to make woman as a by-product of man. *There was no concept of conception, no gestation, no fetus, no growth in uterus, no birth.* Rather the job was done by fiat: Let there be! The stupendous ability of the working god was stressed and made to appear natural, smooth and uninterrupted.[5] (Emphasis added.)

I think we have to ask ourselves, Who profits from such a myth?

The Genesis myth establishes a hierarchical structure of inequality and legitimates the temporal priority and higher status of the male. It "de-births" the origin of the human species by taking away woman as birth-giver. It demotes the earth as the source of life itself. In the Genesis myth the ontological priority belongs to a male spiritual deity, and the earth has all of the status of potter's clay, which has even been produced by a magician-creator out of nothing! And when the world has been produced, it and all its creatures are firmly placed under the foot of the male who is to reign on earth as the male deity already reigns in heaven. Who but males does such a myth benefit? And as the sociologist Peter Berger pointed out in *The Sacred Canopy,* there is a close relationship between what is viewed as the order of things in the heavens and what is viewed as the legitimate or rightful order of things below on earth.

Our Myths Are Male Myths, Not Human Myths

I am told that "there is a universality in myths—a plot which seems to recur over and over again.... There is the *Call to Adventure,* where the hero is drawn out of the world of his ordinary experience (e.g., herding pigs) through a *Magical Threshold* (the hollow trunk of an old tree) into a new extraordinary place. Here he must set out upon the *Road of Trials* (climb the Glass Mountain) in order to gain access to the *Lady* (witch or beautiful princess). He confronts and comes to peace with the *Father* (King), is given (or steals) the Boon (Golden Egg, elixir of life), and *Returns* to the realm of ordinary life to *Transform* it."[6]

These myths obviously arise from the psyche of the male. They express his sense of the heroic life he would aspire to. Yet we have never seen them as male myths but as human myths. We have seldom asked how mythology as well as cultural life in general has been designed by the male quite unself-consciously as an expression of male needs, male anxieties, male pretensions and male idealizations. So, for example, in 1976 a new book about the human body's immune system was given by the author and publisher the title *The Body Is the Hero*. They apparently were oblivious to the fact that for one-half of the human race, the body is not the hero.

"Is Female to Male as Nature Is to Culture?"

With the maleness of culture in mind, it now seems appropriate to reexamine even the basic distinction between culture and nature, a distinction which has nearly always been made in a hierarchical fashion with culture assumed superior to nature.

Consider first the distinction between "culture" and "nature" that seems to exist in every society. A group of female anthropologists at Stanford University has addressed this and related questions in *Woman, Culture and Society*. In an overview of the book Michelle Zimbalist Rosaldo reminds us of the "domestic" orientation of women due to childbearing and childrearing. She contrasts this with the "public" orientation of men, who are free to organize the "activities, institutions, and forms of association that link, rank, organize, or subsume particular mother-child groups."[7] It is men who are free to create "those broader associations that we call 'society,' universalistic systems of order, meaning, and commitment that link particular mother-child groups."[8]

Culture or society, then, is a product of the non-domestic life of the men. The view of reality projected by a men's culture can then be expected to "tilt" reality according to the way life is perceived by men.

In "Is Female to Male as Nature Is to Culture?" Sherry B. Ortner assumes that culture is created by "rising above nature." "Every culture, or generically, 'culture' is engaged in the process of generating and sustaining systems of meaningful form (symbols, artifacts, etc.) by means of which humanity transcends the givens of natural existence, bends them to its purposes, controls them in its interests."[9] She argues that since culture automatically sees itself as "above" nature, women universally have an inferior status because, in their involvement with menstruation, childbearing, and childrearing, they seem closer to nature and thus are "pulled down" in status.

But just suppose that Sherry Ortner has the situation reversed. *Could it be that nature is "pulled down" in status because of its psycho-sexual linkage with women, especially Mother?.* Certainly Becker illustrates such a linkage.

"Mother Nature"

Let us consider for a moment our feminizing of nature as "Mother Nature." I have found it fascinating to read John Passmore's book *Man's Responsibility for Nature* where in a very scholarly interpretation he studiously and consistently avoids ever sexualizing (feminizing) nature and discusses nature always as an "it." Yet many of those whom Passmore has chosen to quote slip quite unconsciously into feminine portrayals of nature ("virgin resources," and so on).

Examples abound. Passmore quotes Fichte as saying "Nature shall ever become more and more intelligible and transparent even in *her* most secret depths; human power, enlightened and armed by human invention, shall *rule over her* without difficulty."[10] (Emphasis added.) He quotes W. A. Gauld as saying "Man has implanted so much of his own design that he appears less a subject of Nature's decrees than a partner who enables *her to reveal new amplitudes* of power, to render new services to material well-being, and not without *grace and beauty to share with Man* the great experiment of life."[11] (Emphasis added.)

Passmore quotes Edward Malins as calling "Nature...a raw goddess"[12] and George Perkins Marsh as saying "The ravages committed by man subvert the relations and destroy the balance which nature has established between *her* organized [*sic.* "organic"?] and *her* inorganic creations; and *she* avenges herself upon the intruder, by letting loose upon *her* defaced provinces...."[13] (Emphasis added.)

Passmore quotes others and then, either not noticing or ignoring their feminizing of nature, he resumes his own completely neuter approach. Only when the context demands it does Passmore permit himself a sexualization of nature:

Man does not, on this view, "rape nature." Rather, to continue the metaphor, he seeks to gain intellectual knowledge of her, overcoming her resistance not by force but by his intimate knowledge of her secrets, by seduction.[14]

*   *   *

We shall begin, rather, with the principal accusation—that Western attitudes to nature are infected with "arrogance," an arrogance which has continued into the post-Christian world and makes men think of nature as a "captive to be raped" rather than as a "partner to be cherished."[15]

How can it be that Passmore can use so many quotations which do feminize nature, as well as occasional quotes which use the potent metaphor of "rape," and yet never think to raise the question of the relationships in men's minds and psyches between nature and the feminine?

During a recent trip to Iceland I was struck by an outdoor larger-than-life statue done by Iceland's outstanding sculptor Asmundur Sveinsson. It portrays a large bosomy woman bending nude over a toddler who is sitting up sucking on one breast while the mother-figure indulgently is kissing the child's head. Inside the sculptor's studio there is a small model of the finished statue labeled "Mother Earth." I thought to myself, How incredible!—here it is—the ultimate portrait of Mother Nature!

The Sense of Nature as Inexhaustible Mother

The psychologist Dorothy Dinnerstein in her pioneering book *The Mermaid and the Minotaur (1976)* is clear that the male psyche makes a crucial connection between the primal parent (female) and the rest of nature. She cites Margaret Mead[16] and H. R. Hays,[17] among others, as having "documented the tendency, expressed by people under a wide range of cultural conditions, to see in woman a mystic continuity with non-human processes like rain and the fertility of plants."[18]

Our difficulty in coming to grasp the fact of the mother's separate human subjectivity (like our related difficulty in outgrowing the early feeling that she is omnipotent and responsible for every blessing and curse of existence) has central consequences not only for the way we look at women, but also for our stance toward nature. Because the early mother's boundaries are so indistinct, the non-human surround with which she merges takes on some of her own quasi-personal quality. In our failure to distinguish clearly between her and nature, we assign to each properties that belong to the other: We cannot believe how accidental, unconscious, unconcerned—i.e., unmotherly nature really is; and we cannot believe how vulnerable, conscious, autonomously wishful—i.e., human—the early mother really was.

Our over-personification of nature, then, is inseparable from our under-personification of woman. We cannot listen to reason when it tells us that the mother—who was once continuous with nature—is a fully sentient fellow person; nor can we listen when it tells us that nature—which was once continuous with the mother—is wholly impersonal, non-sentient. *If we could outgrow our feeling that the first parent was semi-human, a force of nature, we might also be able to outgrow the idea that nature is semi-human, and our parent.*[19] (Emphasis added.)

*   *   *

Inextricable from the notion that nature is our semi-sentient early mother is the notion that she is inherently inexhaustible, that if she does not provide everything we would like to have it is because she does not want to, that her treasure is infinite and can if necessary be taken by force. This view of Mother Earth is in turn identical with the view of woman as Earth Mother, a bottomless source of richness, a being not human enough to have needs of an importance as primary, as self-evident, as the importance of our own needs, but voluntary and conscious enough so that if she does not give us what we expect she is withholding it on purpose and we are justified in getting it from her any way we can. The murderous infantilism of our relation to nature follows inexorably from the murderous infantilism of our sexual arrangements. To outgrow the one we must outgrow the other.[20] (Emphasis added.)

Men's exploitation of Mother Nature has so far been kept in check largely by their conception of the practical risk they themselves ran in antagonizing, depleting, spoiling her. (In preliterate societies, we are told, ritual apologies are offered by hunters to the animals they kill, and by woodcutters to the spirits who inhabit the trees they chop down.) As technology has advanced, and they have felt more powerful, one part of this sense of risk—the fear of antagonizing her—has abated. A euphoric sense of conquest has replaced it: the son has set his foot on the mother's chest, he has harnessed her firmly to his uses, he has opened her body once and for all and may now help himself at will to its riches. What remains is the danger that she will be depleted, spoiled. Men's view of this danger has been fatally short-sighted; it has not kept pace with the actual growth of their destructive power. What has kept it so short-sighted has been, at least in part, the strength of their vindictive, grabby feelings. To maintain a longer, more enlightened view, these feelings—unleashed by their sense of conquest—would at this point have to be pulled back in, and kept under control, by a more powerful effort of will than they seem to be able to muster.[21]

Perhaps because of the psychological realities Dinnerstein describes, mythic consciousness throughout the ages has closely linked Earth/Mother/Sex/Death. "...The Great Goddess had several faces," writes William Irwin Thompson, "she was huge and called us from her womb, she was beautiful and called us to her bed, and she was ugly and called us to death."[22] "The concommitant of birth is death," writes Fontaine Belford. "And to the mythic imagination they have both come into the world through woman. The earth is a 'maternal mouth that spits out and sucks back in forever' (Helen Diver, *Mothers and Amazons*, p. 20). The earth may be the womb from which all life springs; it is also the tomb to which all life returns."[23] This fear may be accentuated in the life of the male because only he experiences the loss of semen as well as the loss of erection within the vaginal mouth of the female.

The various ways in which we all, females as well as males, at times feminize nature suggests a very fundamental question: *Is there something about our very human dependence upon nature which reminds us all of our early dependence upon our physical mothers? And, if this is so, what are the emotional or psychic consequences of this resemblance?*

The Infant's Sense of Oneness with Mother

The anthropologist Nancy Chodorow writes about infantile dependence and the dawn of identity in her article "Family Structure and Feminine Personality":

> All children begin life in a state of "infantile dependence"... upon an adult or adults, in most cases their mother. This state consists first in the persistence of primary identification with the mother: the child does not differentiate herself/himself from her/his mother but experiences a sense of oneness with her.[24]

I would underscore this perception that *both* sexes begin in a state of primary identification with the female parent. However, I would want to go a good bit further and point out that the experiences of the two sexes differ sharply when a child begins to develop its own separate identity, as well as its own gender identity. Girls discover that they have made their primary identification with someone of the *same* sex. Girls are thus encouraged to *continue* modeling themselves after the female. The consequences which follow from this state of affairs are, in my view, most important.

The Special Psychic Predicament of the Boy-Child

Consider the difficulty faced by the boy-child. He finds that his early primal-identification with the mother-figure is an identification with the wrong sex. Furthermore, his potential male model is mostly absent—and thus invisible—whether (as in primitive times) off hunting or (today) off working in factory or bureaucracy. But even this does not totally encompass the boy-child's problem, for *he has not only made his primal and most tender identification with someone of the other sex but with someone of the (female) sex that is treated as "nigger."*

A parallel to the psychic predicament of the boy-child can be found in Lillian Smith's *Killers of the Dream*. Lillian Smith tells of the psychic tensions experienced by white children growing up in the Old South where young whites were often raised from a very early age by mothering black women. These children would form deep emotional attachments with their mammie—only to discover that within the caste system of the South she was a "nigger." To grow up white in that society they had to distance themselves emotionally from what was a primal tender identification and disown their own deepest emotional attachment.

> ... This dual relationship which so many white southerners have had with two mothers, one white and one colored and each of a different culture that centered in different human values, makes the Oedipus complex seem by comparison almost a simple adjustment.... Before the ego had gained strength, just as he is reaching out to make his first ties with the human family, this small white child learns to love both mother and nurse.... Strong bonds begin to grow as the most profound relationships of his life are formed, holding him to two women whose paths will take them far from each other.... Because white mother has always set up right and wrong, has with authority established the "do" and the "don't" of behavior, his conscience, as it grows in him, ties its allegiance to her and to the white culture and authority which she and his father represent.
>
> Big white house, little cabin, enter the picture he is slowly forming in his mind about this strange world he lives in, and both begin subtly to give pattern to it. A separation has begun, a crack that extends deep into his personality. He erects "white" image-ideals and secretly pulls them down again. He says aloud what his heart denies stubbornly. Part of him stays more and more in the world he "belongs" in; part of him stays forever in the world he dare not acknowledge. He feels deep tenderness for his colored nurse and pleasure in being with her, but he begins to admire more and more the lovely lady who is his "real" mother.... However they dealt with it, nearly all men—and

women—of the dominant class in the South suffered not only the usual painful experiences of growing up in America but this special Southern trauma in which segregation not only divided the races but divided the white child's heart.[25]

What Lillian Smith describes seems to me an exact parallel to what the male child experiences when he is "mothered" by a woman and then must strive to grow up male in a society which denigrates the female. He too resolves this deep psychic tension and separation by repressing and rejecting that part of himself which *is* tender and emotional and dependent and rooted in those deep recesses of his earliest life and memories.

Male as "Not-Female"

Nancy Chodorow has written about the boy-child's response to this earliest identity crisis:

A boy, in his attempt to gain an elusive masculine identification, often comes to define this masculinity largely in negative terms, as that which is not feminine or involved with women.... Internally, the boy tries to reject his mother and deny his attachment to her and the strong dependence upon her that he still feels. He also tries to deny the deep personal identification with her that has developed during his early years. He does this by repressing whatever he takes to be feminine inside himself, and, importantly, *by denigrating and devaluing whatever he considers to be feminine in the outside world.* As a societal member, he also appropriates to himself and defines as superior particular social activities and cultural (moral, religious, and creative) spheres—possibly in fact, "society"...and "culture" ...themselves.[26] (Emphasis added.)

I regard the boy-child's response to his earliest identity crisis as being of critical importance to our understanding of the psychosexual development of males—and to our understanding of the psychodynamics at work in the cultures which males create. So in what follows, I am going to consider each of the boy-child responses Nancy Chodorow describes. I will also cite substantiating evidence from other widely varied sources.

The first response of the boy-child is to try to define his masculinity in negative terms. His problem is one of wresting a male identity for himself out of an earlier period of helpless dependence upon mother. His identity has been blurred and his selfhood merged with hers. "Men learn from the time they're boys," Warren Farrell says, "that the worst possible thing is to be considered feminine—a 'sissy.' *The male's fear that he might be thought of as a female—with all the negative implications that carries—has been the central basis of his need to prove himself masculine.*"[27] (Emphasis added.)

"Not-Dependent" Equals "Masculine"

This assertion by the boy-child of his own identity is a separation and drawing apart in an attempt to delineate himself as not dependent, and thus masculine. He resists feelings of weakness or vulnerability or dependence. Such feelings are repressed and denied, because they would evoke memories of his earlier dependence. His neurotic fear is that such "baby" feelings will pull him back to baby-like dependencies—and a man is "not a baby." Marc Feigen Fasteau is a young lawyer who in his book *The Male Machine* writes about this male problem with feelings of dependence:

> What is particularly difficult for men is seeking or accepting help from friends. I, for one, learned early that dependence was unacceptable. . . . "You can't express dependence when you feel it," a corporate executive said, "because it's a kind of absolute. If you are loyal 90% of the time and disloyal 10%, would you be considered loyal? Well, the same happens with independence: you are either dependent or independent; you can't be both."
>
> "Feelings of dependence," another explained, "are identified with weakness or 'untoughness' and our culture doesn't accept those things in men."[28]

Such ambivalence about dependent feelings has enormous psycho-sexual repercussions both for males' relationships with females and also, of course, for their relationship with whatever they perceive as feminine, *Is it possible then for men to think clearly and feel positively about our human dependence upon the ecosystems of the biosphere (i.e., upon nature) if they have not resolved in a satisfactory way their basic psycho-sexual conflict about feelings of dependence and weakness?* I would suggest not.

The Cult of Toughness

Marc Feigen Fasteau has written about the effect in the Vietnam-War period of hang-ups about "tough" masculinity and about not being dependent. He cites David Halberstam's account of the behavior of U.S. political leaders in that period:

> He [President Lyndon B. Johnson] had always been haunted by the idea that he would be judged as being insufficiently manly for the job, that he would lack courage at a crucial moment. More than a little insecure himself, he wanted very much to be seen as a man; it was a conscious thing. . . . He had unconsciously divided people around him between men and boys. Men were activists, doers, who conquered business empires, who acted instead of talked, who made it in the world of other men and had the respect of other men. Boys were the talkers and the writers and the intellectuals, who sat around thinking and criticizing and doubting instead of doing. . . .
>
> *   *   *
>
> As Johnson weighed the advice he was getting on Vietnam, it was the boys who were most skeptical, and the men who were most sure and confident and hawkish and who had Johnson's respect. Hearing that one member of his Administration was becoming a dove on Vietnam, Johnson said, "Hell, he has to squat to piss." The men had, after all, done things in their lifetimes, and they had the respect of other men. Doubt itself, he thought, was almost a feminine quality, doubts were for women; once, on another issue, when Lady Bird raised her doubts, Johnson had said of course she was doubtful, it was like a woman to be uncertain.[29] (Emphasis added.)

Is it disturbing to realize how early psychic conflicts remain unresolved in our leaders—and affect decisions involving death and life for thousands of human beings? Fasteau summarizes his view of the effects of the "cult of toughness" upon U.S. foreign policy in that period:

> In short, Presidents Kennedy, Johnson and Nixon and their advisors drew an analogy between the politics of the fifties [the McCarthy era] and the politics of the sixties without examining the realities of either. This failure of analysis and the readiness to believe that the right, which might accuse them of being too soft and weak if they withdrew from Vietnam, had great political power, was in large part the result of their personal preoccupation with toughness and the projection of that preoccupation onto the voting public.[30]

As Eugene Bianchi has so aptly observed, "Deliberation and decision at the top take place in a male lodge where the cultural myths of masculinity reign supreme."[31]

Such unexamined, unfaced, unresolved fears about dependence, weakness, and masculine identity will also plague us when we try to acknowledge our human dependence upon natural ecosystems. My own observations are like Fasteau's: men do not like to feel dependent or acknowledge feeling dependent. Feeling dependent resonates for them as-yet-unresolved emotional issues. It seems in some strange way to remind them of that powerful and infantile relationship to mother—and this they fear.

Rituals of Growing Up

Such attitudes did not spring Athena-like full-blown out of the forehead of Zeus in the adulthood of men like Kennedy and Johnson. Such a masculine mystique has to be carefully taught (as indeed it is) by all the nuances and rituals of "growing up male" in America. Biographical accounts in *Straight/White/Male*[32] and essays in *Men and Masculinity*[33] document the extent of these insistent social pressures upon boys and men to "prove" their masculinity by being tough. Eugene Bianchi also analyzes these pressures which pervade boyhood and continue in adulthood to structure the life of the male:

> Big-time football manifests and reinforces the ideal of masculine identity through its aggressive ethos. The real man is aggressive and dominant in all situations. The weekend trek to the arena is not an escape from the world of corporate America; rather it is a weekly pilgrimage to the national shrines where the virtues of toughness and insensitivity can be renewed.[34]

> *   *   *

> Although we don't want to acknowledge it, rape is the prototype example of the masculine game that pervades society. The competitor, the opponent, the enemy needs to be reduced, humiliated, made powerless, made into woman.[35]

> *   *   *

> The male psychic patterns at work in rape are also disclosed, though in more refined and respectable ways, in economic life. I am not only referring to the financial rapaciousness of the criminal underworld, sometimes called the Mafia, but rather to the legal structures and dynamics of our capitalist system where masculine self-identity and value are closely linked to performing according to an intense, competitive code. The motivating ideal of the hero/hunter capitalist is to become worthy by maximizing profits, by amassing ever more wealth. This ideal calls for the virtues of toughness, aggressiveness and a willingness to sacrifice mere humanistic considerations for technological efficiency and material gain....I submit that the fundamental impulse of our economic system is rapacious at home and abroad because such "rape" fulfills male ego-needs conditioned by our culture.[36]

Wife as Mother-in-Chains

Any wife will tell you that within the marriage relationship men are very dependent in certain ways. "He's just like a baby when he gets sick." "He couldn't boil water for himself." "I have to be so careful of his male ego." "He needs me to bolster him up when he's down." "He's so vulnerable inside but he won't let anyone else see it."

Isn't this dependence? Ah yes, but dependence-with-a-crucial-difference. It is dependence not upon a powerful female mother-figure but dependence within a dominant/submissive relationship and involves dependence upon an impotent, non-threatening female figure known in our culture as a "wife." A patriarchal culture programs a wife to be submissive, to be economically impotent, and in many other ways to be inferior and non-threatening to her man. In short, a wife is to be *below* her man, not above.

Warren Farrell has characterized women's support of male egos: "Women are the jockstraps of the world. They are always supporting us, but never quite showing. The real and metaphorical jockstraps protect the two most fragile parts of the male anatomy."[37] Dorothy Dinnerstein points out that—

...[W]hile man takes over her overt power, as protecting and providing despot, woman as food preparer continues literally to feed him, as body servant goes on grooming him, as housekeeper maintains for him the comforting surround over which he, however, formally presides: again, her old services are made available with the old indignities and risks deleted, indeed to some degree reversed.[38]

*   *   *

...A naturally keen childhood fantasy-wish (lived out widely by adult men with the women whom they rule) is to keep female will in live captivity, obediently energetic, fiercely protective of its captor's pride, ready always to vitalize his projects with its magic maternal blessing and to support them with its concrete, self-abnegating maternal help.[39]

This male dependence upon a wife's non-threatening and submissive support of her man is an understandable development, when it is viewed against the psycho-sexual backdrop of Nancy Chodorow's boy-child in search of an "elusive masculine identity." After the boy denies his dependence upon his mother—repressing whatever *inside* himself he feels is feminine (the weakness, the softness, the doubts, the uncertainties Fasteau describes)—then at the same time, Nancy Chodorow points out, the boy also feels it necessary to be "denigrating and devaluing whatever he considers to be feminine in the *outside* world."[40] (Emphasis added.) This is clearly visible, for example, in the scorn of girl-toys, girl-ways, and girl-attributes among preschool-age boys as young as three years.

This is the psychological need—what I have been calling the psycho-sexual root—that underlies the inferior and submissive status assigned to females. The societies that assign females this status are societies which are the product of men's freedom from childcare; where women and men share equally in the childcare, the status of women is not inferior. The cultures referred to are the Ilongots in the Philippines and the Mbuti pygmies of Africa and the Arapesh in New Guinea. "The most egalitarian societies are not those in which male and female are opposed or are even competitors, but those in which men value and participate in the domestic life of the home. Correspondingly, they are societies in which women can readily participate in important public events."[41]

The Mastery of Mother Nature

It is important for us to see that men have done with Mother Nature this same dominance/submission flip-flop. They have by their technologies worked steadily and for generations to transform a psychologically intolerable dependence upon a seemingly powerful and capricious "Mother Nature" into a soothing and acceptable dependence upon a subservient and non-threatening "wife." This "need to be above" and to dominate permeates male attitudes toward nature. It is as though men did not like *any* feelings of depending upon "Mother Nature." Nature must be below, just as Wife must be below, for to be a man *a man must be in control*!

5.

The Threat of Death
and the Appeal of Mastery

The Hurricane

The hurricane came last night. It had been raining for three straight days and everything was damp and sodden when yesterday morning we learned from the radio that the storm was indeed heading up the coast and straight toward us. Everyone within five hundred yards of the shoreline was being advised to evacuate before the storm struck. So the day was spent in frantic preparations for the storm. An extra high lunar tide would crest about midnight at about the expected arrival time of the center of the hurricane.

On the beach figures draped in slickers or wet to the skin were laboring to bring in several heavier sailboats and pull them over rollers across beach and lawn to waiting boat trailers. The raft that on pleasanter summer days had been for sunning and swimming now had to be pulled in and secured as best they could. The winds that were expected could move and hurl anything not fastened down, so porch furniture, trash barrels, window boxes, awnings, everything was brought into the living room. An expected tidal surge of ten to fourteen feet above high tide had been announced so the basement level that faced out onto the lawn and beach had to be surveyed for what could be removed to the crowded safety of upstairs. Then quickly the heavy hurricane shutters were pounded into place over the beachside windows and doors. The radio told of traffic jams as people tried to evacuate and the Civil Defense announced evacuation centers. We had the kerosene and lanterns out, and a hurried trip early in the day brought fresh batteries, some dry ice, and a few replacement canned goods.

Finally we sat down for a last supper while we discussed where to go to evacuate. Should we stay with a friend in the city? Or can we share in the excitement and danger and watch the storm's coming? We compromise and go to a friend's house that perches high on a bluff above the water and storm. We pack quickly and wonder what we will find when we return in the morning. At the friend's house we admire the large ocean-view windows and watch the rising waters and winds which darkness will soon hide from us.

By eleven o'clock the winds really begin. We can hear their shrill whistle up and down the chimney and feel the tug of their power as the massive overhanging deck begins to shake slightly with the strongest gusts. Everyone is getting into slickers again to go outside now to experience better the full force of the storm. A teenager observes that he may never be in another hurricane and that he wants to *feel* this one! So wrapped in slickers we slip out a side door and staying close to the house we turn the corner into the slashing rain and wind and the crashing roar of waves.

The wind is blowing so hard you can lean with all your weight into it and not fall down. Giant waves are rolling in, crashing again and again and again against the seawall and casting spray upward into the winds. We estimate the wind as about sixty miles an hour now, and we know the eye of the storm has not yet come. But it is time for the tide to be turning. The storm is late. And we know now that we will be spared the conjunction of high tide and the worst of the storm. The tidal surge almost certainly won't come.

Back inside the electricity flickers and then fades. We scurry for candles and gather around the battery radio as people all up and down the coast phone the local station about trees down, electricity gone, high water marks, and wind directions at different locations. It is somehow comforting to have the communication of phone and radio as the power of the storm isolates everyone in their homes. The candlelight is soft on our faces as drowsiness overtakes us about 3 A.M. and we begin to curl up with the dog and the cats against each other. We stir ourselves and get to bed. As we lie in bed the house is shaking slightly with the wind gusts, and we wonder what may happen to the large old tree we know is almost dancing to the wind overhead.

We awaken in a few hours. It is a windy morning but the rain has gone and the wind has shifted into the west. We dress and eat quickly for we are anxious to explore the aftermath of the storm. The girls are still asleep but we find the boys are already out and come back with reports of trees down and moorings dragged and two boats totally destoyed. The water and the shore are littered with debris from broken docks and rafts, and lawns have gone from lush green to dead grass. Everyone is out inspecting; there is a camaraderie after a storm as we congratulate and commiserate. There are several huge trees uprooted, ripped up like giant onions, exposing six to ten inch thick taproots which have snapped in two. One wonders why some trees bend and survive, and others are ripped up or simply broken. The capacity to bend with the violence of nature, to batten down the hatches and retreat like a turtle within your shell—or to sway and dance and move within the wind as the trees do which survive—these are valuable capacities for humans to have. Why is it that we feel sometimes that we must confront nature, as with a gun, standing up to do battle and seeking to conquer, when it would be more appropriate to shutter and bend? In his pioneering book *Design with Nature* Ian McHarg contrasts these two ways of meeting the violence of the sea:

> In their long dialogue with the sea the Dutch have learned that it cannot be stopped but merely directed or tempered, and so they have always selected flexible construction. Their dikes are not made as are our defenses, with reinforced concrete. Rather they are constructed with layers of fascines—bundles of twigs—laid on courses of sand and clay, the whole of which is then armored with masonry. The dunes, stabilized with grasses, provide an even greater flexibility than dikes, accepting the waves but reducing their velocity and absorbing the muted forces. In contrast concrete walls invite the full force of the waves and finally succumb to the undercutting of the insidious sea. The Dutch dikes are fitting.[1]

The Need to Control

The male need to control and dominate has been little examined by our male-dominated culture and male-dominated psychology. It has been accepted as a natural and necessary human instinct, but one that is magically present in one half of the human race and magically missing in the other half, except for a few perverted, disturbed, aggressive, dominating females who got some of the magic potion by mistake!

As we look at others in the animal kingdom, we can speculate that this male need to dominate may be a hold-over from primate behavior. Carl Sagan, writing about the evolution of human intelligence, tells us:

> Squirrel monkeys with "gothic" facial markings have a kind of ritual or display which they perform when greeting one another. The males bare their teeth, rattle the bars of their cage, utter a high-pitched squeak, which is possibly terrifying to squirrel monkeys, and lift their legs to exhibit an erect penis. While such behavior would border on impoliteness at many contemporary human social gatherings, it is a

fairly elaborate act and serves to maintain dominance hierarchies in squirrel-monkey communities....

The connection between sexual display and position in a dominance hierarchy can be found frequently among the primates. Among Japanese macaques, social class is maintained and reinforced by daily mounting: Males of lower caste adopt the characteristic submissive sexual posture of the female in oestrus and are briefly and ceremonially mounted by higher-caste males. These mountings are both common and perfunctory. They seem to have little sexual content but rather serve as easily understood symbols of who is who in a complex society....

In a television interview in 1976, a professional football player was asked by the talk-show host if it was embarrassing for football players to be together in the locker room with no clothes on. His immediate response: "We strut! No embarrassment at all. It's as if we're saying to each other, 'Let's see what you got, man!'—except for a few, like the specialty team members and the water boy."[2]

Charles Ferguson in *The Male Attitude* puts the control and dominance issue in interesting historical perspective:

What was involved in both the slave question and in the revolt against Britain was the whole doctrine of control.... It was not merely that some men favored slavery and some did not; that some wanted to rebel against British rule and some wanted to remain loyal. The thing that mattered was that the emotion of the total society in America revolved around questions of status and dominance and control.[3]

The Desire for Mastery

Writing from a very different perspective Langdon Winner in *Autonomous Technology* is very clear that science and technology have been focused upon control:

The concern of science and technology with the possibilities of control have often found expression in terms which closely parallel the language of politics. This is perhaps not surprising if one rcalls that both politics and technics have as their central focus the sources and exercise of power. Our thinking about technology, however, seems inextricably bound to a single conception of the manner in which power is used—the style of absolute mastery, the despotic, one-way control of the master over the slave. Other notions central to the historical discussion of political power—membership, participation, and authority founded on consent—seem to have no relevance in this sphere. In our traditional ways of thinking, the concept of mastery and the master-slave metaphor are the dominant ways of describing man's relationship to nature, as well as to the implements of technology.

*   *   *

The theme of mastery in the literature of technology is even more evident with regard to Western man's relationship to nature. Here there are seldom any reservations about man's rightful role in conquering, vanquishing, and subjugating everything natural. This is his power and his glory....Nature is the universal prey, to manipulate as humans see fit.

In no place is this theme more clearly stated than in the writings of the most famous early advocate of a world-transforming scientific revolution, Francis Bacon.

*   *   *

Men shall "obey" nature for as long as it takes to learn her secrets. They will then command her as tyrants once commanded their political subjects. Bacon clearly means to say that this change will benefit the human race not only because science will improve material well-being but also because those who crave power will turn to more "wholesome" pursuits. Apparently an ambitious man must subjugate something. And nature, unlike human beings, will not mind subjugation.[4]

The Dread of Helplessness

The woman psychoanalyst Karen Horney is the only one I know who has analyzed what she calls "The Appeal of Mastery." In *Neurosis and Human Growth* she says that this kind of neurotic individual has both a "superior proud self" and a "despised self":

If he experiences himself as a superior being, he tends to be expansive in his strivings and his belief about what he can achieve; he tends to be more or less openly arrogant, ambitious, aggressive and demanding; he feels self-sufficient; he is disdainful of others; he requires admiration or blind obedience.

*   *   *

In the expansive solution [of these two neurotic selfhoods] *the individual prevailingly identifies himself with his glorified self.* When speaking of "himself" he means, with Peer Gynt, his very grandiose self. Or, as one patient put it, "I exist only as a superior being."

*   *   *

The feeling of superiority that goes with this solution is not necessarily conscious but—whether conscious or not—largely determines behavior, strivings, and attitudes toward life in general. The appeal of life lies in its *mastery. It chiefly entails his determination, conscious or unconscious, to overcome every obstacle—in or outside himself—and the belief that he should be able, and in fact is able, to do so.* He should be able to master the adversities of fate, the difficulties of a situation, the intricacies of intellectual problems, the resistances of other people, conflicts in himself. [When I listen to these words of Karen Horney, I cannot help but hear also the male voices in our contemporary scene insisting that they *can* handle nuclear power without disaster, they *can* find a solution for radioactive nuclear waste, they *can* do recombinant DNA research without imperiling all of us.] *The reverse side of the necessity for mastery is his dread of anything connoting helplessness; this is the most poignant dread he has.*[5] (Emphasis added.)

In the sexual realm such a compelling need to "master" situations and challenges would obviously result in viewing the female as submissive and compliant, and *needing* her to be such in order that he can continue in what he sees as essential for his selfhood, namely, mastery. A book about sexual love advised in 1973 that "Every sexual encounter must be a pitched battle betweeen your sureness and her timidity. . . . *What you want is automatically best for her*. . . . Nothing is more pitiful, pathetic, and even contemptible than a man who yields his position of masculinity to his woman. He is abandoning his fight and allowing himself to be led by his woman—something which no normal man can ever possibly tolerate. . . . She wants to be a woman—and she can only be a woman if you are *really a man.*"[6] (Emphasis added.) As David Halberstam and Marc Feigen Fasteau have pointed out, it is not just in bed that the male in our culture is haunted by the compelling need to be "really a man." Fasteau writes that "the feeling that the United States must at all costs avoid 'the humiliation of defeat' is the unarticulated major premise of nearly every document."[7]

So is there any way that some of these same psycho-sexual drives can *not* also be operative when "men" view nature? Rebelling against any dependence upon "Mother Nature," he must of necessity put "her" down into the dominated, submissive compliant-wife and sexual-woman role. Like the sexologist, he easily convinces himself that *"What you want is automatically best for her."* because nothing he can imagine would be worse than if Man lost his sense that his is the control or mastery of the situation on earth.

Death and the Heroic "Proving Oneself a Man"

The heroic mode is closely allied to the need to master and to conquer. All are expressions of the masculine that are commonly found in patriarchal (male-dominated) cultures. In countless myths and stories the strong man is portrayed as struggling against a problem—nature, fate, countless "odds" that are against him—struggling to overcome and prove himself "a hero." In the challenge-and-response syndrome of the heroic mode, mountains exist to be climbed, problems exist to be solved, records exist in order to be broken, obstacles are to be overcome.

This pervasive heroic stance Ernest Becker finds rooted in "man's" questioning of "his" value in the universe:

> In childhood we see the struggle for self-esteem at its least disguised....They so openly express man's tragic destiny: he must desperately justify himself as an object of primary value in the universe; he must stand out, be a hero, make the biggest possible contribution to world life, show that he *counts* more than anything or anyone else.[8] (Emphasis added.)

Becker continues with the varied ways in which this heroic need for "proving oneself" is manifest:

> It doesn't matter whether the cultural hero system is frankly magical, religious, and primitive or secular, scientific, and civilized. It is still *a mythical hero-system in which people serve in order to earn a feeling of primary value, of cosmic specialness, of ultimate usefulness to creation, of unshakable meaning.* They earn this feeling by carving out a place in nature, by building an edifice that reflects human value: a temple, a cathedral, a totem pole, a skyscraper, a family that spans three generations. The hope and belief is that the things that man creates in society are of lasting worth and meaning, that they outlive or outshine death and decay, that man and his products count.[9] (Emphasis added.)

Becker finds this heroic need to prove oneself and count for something is human and rooted in the human fear of death. I find it male—and see the heroic need to prove oneself rooted in the male envy of the female's sense of intrinsic worth which needs no proving and which is based upon childbearing. Let us examine this alternative to Becker's interpretation of the heroic.

The Heroic Impulse and Males' Envy of Women

The male envy and dread of the fertile woman is rarely discussed in psychoanalytic circles. Freud made a great deal of penis-envy, but he never seemed to have perceived the existence of "uterus envy," although Bruno Bettelheim is very clear in *Symbolic Wounds* (1962) that there is a lot of evidence that such exists:

Parallel to women's envy is the desire of men to possess female genitals in addition to their own....We have observed similar desires, though less frankly expressed, in adolescent boys.

*   *   *

Each of these boys stated repeatedly, independently of the other and to different persons, that he felt it was "a cheat" and "a gyp" that he did not have a vagina.

*   *   *

We are hardly in need of proof that men stand in awe of the procreative power of women, that they wish to participate in it, and that both emotions are found readily in Western society.[10]

David Riesman, in reviewing Bettelheim's book, comments:

On the whole, men, by virtue of the very patriarchal dominance which puts them on top, must repress the extent of their longings for the simplicities and indisputable potentialities of being a woman, whereas women are much freer to express their envy of the male's equipment and roles.[11]

Bettelheim's thesis is that in more primitive cultures this male envy of the procreative power of women is not repressed but is expressed in the initiation ceremonies of the young boy into manhood, which incise the penis so that it bleeds in imitation of the female's menstruation.

Rivalry with Women as Goad to Male Achievement

Karen Horney goes beyond Bettelheim's description of males' envy of women to talk about males' "dread of women." This dread of women she sees as "an immense incitement" for male achievement:

Mother goddesses are earthy goddesses, fertile like the soil. They bring forth new life and they nurture it. It was this life-creating power of woman, an elemental force, that filled man with admiration. And this is exactly the point where problems arise. For it is contrary to human nature to sustain appreciation without resentment toward capabilities that one does not possess. Thus a man's minute share in creating new life became, for him, an immense incitement to create something new on his part. He has created values of which he might well be proud. State, religion, art, and science are essentially his creations, and our entire culture bears the masculine imprint.

*   *   *

Even the greatest satisfactions or achievements, if born out of sublimation, cannot fully make up for something for which we are not endowed by nature. Thus there has remained an obvious residue of general resentment of men against women....hence their tendency to devalue pregnancy and childbirth and to overemphasize male genitality.[12]

The Machine as Male Means of Productivity

Charles Ferguson in *The Male Attitude* sees man's love affair with the machine not only as "the normal outgrowth of man's effort to extend his effect and control over unseen forces" but "the machine actually offered him the possibility that he might create something that had the semblance of a human being."

For all his growing sense of strength and his power to destroy by means of the gun, the male could not get any real satisfaction from producing. A god could, but he couldn't. And a woman could. She could bring forth life, produce it, hand it to him. Of course the male could procreate. He had an essential part in the life process. He could start it, but it was the woman who finished. By the time of the birth act, his role seemed remote and obscure, far away and all but forgot....By means of combat, questing, holding onto his prerogatives, doing things that women were not permitted to do, the male could in some respects escape frustration but he could not fructify.

*   *   *

The machine, if fully developed, offered Man the prospect that he might become as important as woman in the life process. This was part of the vision and the imagination. With the machine he could produce. Like an ancient deity, it would enable him to do what he could not do otherwise. More exciting, it would enable him to feel what he had not been able to feel before. Through the nexus of the machine he could exercise the function of both the male and the female. What the male produced, *he* produced. He himself personally. Except as menials, there would be no woman in the process of production. None at all, at any step, either at the beginning or the end. Men made the machines that made the machines and the machines they made made things that weren't there before. And no woman around, just as there was no man around in any significant way at the birth of a child.[13]

The Polynesian myth of Maui is a fascinating example of how there can exist, all scrambled together, (a) the heroic male challenging death, (b) male envy of the female reproductive power, and (c) the denigration of the female's role in childbearing. The heroic figure is Maui, a strong young man who sets out to conquer death. Death of course is a terrible female ancestress with a mouth like a barracuda! In order to conquer her (Death), Maui must go inside her clad only in his trusty knife, and she will die if he can emerge (return) without waking her.

Unfortunately for Maui his bird companions are overcome with the absurdity of his attempt and they giggle out loud, waking the terrible ancestress, who strangles Maui to death. At the end of this incredible mythic attempt to recreate childbirth, these classic words appear: "*Men* make heirs, but Death carries them off."[14]

Time, Death, and Decay: The Ultimate Challenge to Mastery

Ernest Becker is right. The threat of death does impinge upon the male need for heroic achievement. The male does feel a great need for immortality as he confronts the possibility of death. And he does not, as the woman does, find that need assuaged through his male involvement in the passage of the generations. He desires to leave majestic footprints upon the sands of time, great achievements in business, philosophy, science, government—the public life.

Such a male orientation—which tends to see all of his achievements in the mental or cultural realm and none in the bodily realm—results in a mind/body dualism. As a result death becomes the great threat that reaches out to darken the whole human participation in the body, rather than death being a natural end to a bodily life. Thus the body itself as well as sex, nature, and woman-as-she-intersects-the-life-of-the-body are all tainted with the dark threat of their involvement in mortality and decay. That is precisely Ernest Becker's vision. There must be another way.

6.

Turning to Another Way

In the ancient days a solemn council was called to consider the origin of death. Great men, movers of empires and corporations, assembled to debate the question. "Death came with our bodies," they said. "Our natural world, of which our bodies are a part, is full of death. Only our minds and spirits are immortal, akin to the gods. And that is why we sharpen our minds and toughen our spirits, and gird up the loins of our souls to be heroic, to project such a magnificent trajectory of a life-span that we conquer the ignominy of our beginnings in the blood and humanness of childbirth, and the dependence of childhood, as well as the humiliation of our endings in the weakness of old age and the blotting-out of death."

As the men talked, they paced the floor and filled the air with their dreams of glory. Great martial adventures, great philosophical and theological systems, great scientific and technological advances, achievements of epic proportions were planned and executed with courage and strength and daring which surely would conquer the beginnings and the endings of man. "We are like gods," the men rhapsodized as they erected. "We are a little lower than the angels, and all other creatures who do not erect as we do, are below us and subject to us. All of nature itself, like the ground we walk upon, will reverberate to the majesty of our footprints upon the sands of time."

But a funny thing happened as the men worked. Some of the vast heroic enterprises, instead of conquering death, began to cause it. Toxic substances, iron laws of economics, megaton killbacks, and blank-faced robot machines began to stalk the earth and "hunt for humans" like demented snipers of the rooftop. Benign Mother Nature turned on her children with murderous ferocity, slowly choking off the air and water which had flowed freely from her abused breasts. Men were cast back upon the despised dependence of their infantile memories.

"This is intolerable!" the men cried out. "We cannot live as we desire. We cannot control the world and all that in it lies. If we live like this, we die and the world dies with us. But not to live like this, not to control and subdue the world, is still worse for us than death! What shall we do? Who shall we kill to make it right?

In the silence that followed, an old woman sitting in the corner knitting clothes for her grandchildren finally spoke. "You men live your lives in agonies of striving, you kill and take the world with you. And for what? You do not know who you are. Always you try to escape your bodies, to put down your flesh, to conquer nature, and where does it get you? He who cannot deal with his birth from a woman, cannot deal with his death. Life comes from death, and death is in life. They are all of a piece."

The men stared at her in disbelief. What could this woman, this other-than-man, know of life or death? Only men cast their cosmologies out upon reality; their metaphors of dualism and hierarchy had etched the ontological skies for so long that they seemed embedded in truth itself. Could it be that there was another way to perceive? Another standing point? Could it be that erection itself had betrayed them into thinking linearly about everything? Could it be that they had missed the basic metaphor of life?

"All right," the men taunted her, "you tell us a story. You tell us about the beginning and the ending, and about the meaning of the middle of life. You tell us."

"I am not like you," the old woman said slowly. "I do not tell stories. I see visions. I see that life is not a line but a circle. Why do men imagine for themselves the illusory freedom of a soaring mind, so that the body of nature becomes a cage? 'Tis not true. To be human is to be circled in the cycles of nature, rooted in the processes that nurture us in life, breathing in and breathing out human life just as plants breathe in and out their photosynthesis. Why do men see themselves as apart from this, or above this? Is it that the natural reproductive processes surge so little through their bodies that they cannot feel their unity with nature in their blood and tissue and bones, as women can? Or is it that they so envy and fear women for their more integral part in nature that they seek to escape from both women and nature into a fantasy world of culture which they themselves can control because they made it up?"

The men roared in anger. "How dare you question the world which we have made, woman, you who were not made by God but made from our rib! We have given birth to you! How could we possibly think that we were born of you, or envy you, or fear you? It is against all rational thought!

But the old woman merely looked at them and said, "To be human is to be born, partake of life, and die. Life itself is the gift. It does not have to be wrenched out of shape, trying to deny both the borning and the dying. Women produce children, and they and the children die. But they know that it was good to have lived. Perhaps someday men too can rest upon the affirmation of being, and there find reassurance and an end to their ceaseless striving. Perhaps someday they shall come to know the circle which is the whole— that which validates being-without-achieving, that which allows one to rest and stop running, that which accepts one as a person and not a hero. The sweet nectar of that whole awaits you in the precious flower of the Now, not in your dreams of glory. Perhaps, someday, men will find their humanity, and give up their divinity."

The old woman had finished speaking and there was silence in the great council room. It was a time for silence.

*   *   *

It is time for a new cosmic vision—a new understanding of human life in its home the earth. The American Indians had such an understanding, but we felt that it was primitive, as indeed we felt they were. But theirs was an organic vision of being human, partaking of both life and death, and living at home on their good earth:

> Today is a very good day to die.
> Every living thing is in harmony with me.
> Every voice sings a chorus within me.
> All beauty has come to rest in my eyes.
> All bad thoughts have departed from me.
> Today is a very good day to die.
> My land is peaceful around me.
> My fields have been turned for the last time.
> My house is filled with laughter.
> My children have come home.
> Yes, today is a very good day to die.[1]

*   *   *

> When the hand of winter gives up its grip to the sun
> And the river's hard ice becomes the tongue to spring
> I must go into the earth itself
> To know the source from which I came.
> Where there is a history of leaves
> I lie face down upon the land.

I smell the rich wet earth
Trembling to allow the birth
Of what is innocent and green.
My fingers touch the yielding earth
Knowing that it contains
All previous births and deaths.
I listen to a cry of whispers
Concerning the awakening earth
In possession of itself.
With a branch between my teeth
I feel the growth of trees
Flowing with life born of ancient death.
I cover myself with earth
So that I may know while still alive
How sweet is the season of my time.[2]

Part 2.

Whole and Home Again

7.

Discovering the Connections within the Structure of Reality

There was no moon tonight but starlight instead—and would there be phosphorescence? The water was still as glass with never a ripple. When we walked into it we suddenly became no longer earthbound but found ourselves wading through the Milky Way—yes, there was phosphorescence—and I never saw so much. As long as we moved and created a stir, be it ever so slight, countless stars were there in the water around us. When we stood still they vanished. While we swam myriads of glistening bits tossed off our arms, spread in rolling silver sparks, underwater and on the surface, endless and everywhere.

The separate definition between water, sky, stars, and our two figures swimming seemed to vanish. All merged into one. The whole universe was one, and I felt us lose separate identity and become one with it. In that instant I knew what the mystics mean when they say, "All is one." To be a part of such beauty for a brief moment was a rare and wonderful experience.[1]

Our Bodies and the Body of Life

The new understanding of life must be systemic and inter-connected. It cannot be linear and hierarchical, for the reality of life on earth is a whole, a circle, an interconnected system in which everything has its part to play and can be respected and accorded dignity. It is difficult for us, trained as we have been in the male culture, to understand the order there is in a diversified system which is non-hierarchical. Our human bodies would provide us with a good example of a non-hierarchical system if we would but take off our hierarchical glasses: the nervous system, the circulatory system, the digestive system, the immune system—all are diverse cooperating equalities. Each has its part to play, each needs the activity of all the others. Ronald J. Glasser, writing in *The Body Is the Hero*, describes the body at one point in this way:

58

Our bodies are made up of over a trillion individual cells, all of which have learned through the long process of evolution to work together, to maintain one another, to do what they do and yet support the whole, so that each will in turn be maintained and protected. Our body is like a great movable city, made up of a trillion individuals all with different skills, yet working together. It has its own ventilation and sewage systems, its own telephone and communications network, a billion miles of interconnecting highways and side streets, a system of alleys, its own supermarkets and factories, disposal plants and heating units. All it really needs to keep going are a few basic raw materials to be brought in—sugars, fats, proteins, carbon, hydrogen, oxygen, nitrogen, magnesium, iron, zinc and calcium, and a way of discharging wastes.[2]

What our bodies can do is remind us that we are of this earth, that this is our heritage and our destiny and our glory. If we take off our Ernest Becker glasses, then we can move into the wonder of life shared with each molecule of the earth, as Ronald Glasser suggests in this passage:

The fluids in our bodies mimic the primeval seas in which we began. The concentrations of salts, of sodium, potassium and chloride in our bloodstream, the cobalt, magnesium and zinc in our tissues, are the same as those that existed in the earliest seas.

We still carry those seas within us, and the same chemical battles that were fought in them a billion years ago are being waged today in fighting our infections and controlling our illnesses. . . . Not only does our blood go back to those ancient seas; we are also, literally, children of the earth. The carbon in our bones is the same carbon that forms the rocks of the oldest mountains. The molecules of sugar that flow through our bloodstream once flowed in the sap of now fossilized trees, while the nitrogren that binds together our bones is the same nitrogen that binds the nitrates to the soil. Life has endured as long as it has because it is formed from substances as basic as the earth itself.[3]

Understanding ourselves as "above," "apart," or "beyond" the natural systems of which we are a part has been an aspect of our sickness in the past. "Difficult as it may be to believe," Ronald Glasser writes, "the differences in all living things have only to do with differences in the specific arrangement and sequence of the chemicals that make up their DNA. Its general helical structure, whether in plants or animals, remains the same throughout the living world, a common heritage coming from the same common beginnings."[4] We are connected by our body to the seas, to the air, to the dirt, even to the germs. Penelope Washburn suggests that even our human sensory openness is connection:

I begin with my body. . . . my body is me. I can think of my body as a porous membrane, not separated from the world, as an organic body pulsing. . . opening and closing. . . taking in and giving out. It is like a flower as it turns to the sun, responds to light, growing, absorbing, expelling. . . . I am breathing gently and with such ease. . . until something happens to tense me, and my breath becomes shallow and labored. My skin is open, each of my cells in hair and skin is intimately connected to air, moisture, sun, dirt, hot and cold.[5]

Even the great chasm we have put between life and non-life, living organisms and inert matter, is being bridged. Scientists have found a life form which seems sometimes to be dead and sometimes living. That bridge is the virus. Ronald Glasser writes:

The question remained for decades whether viruses were alive or dead. Today we realize they hold a middle ground. Outside the body, a virus is nonliving—just a tiny crystalline structure, appearing under the electron microscope as nothing more than a minute, sharply etched piece of silica or particle of quartz. It might as well be a piece of organic debris picked off the moon, to be examined here on earth. There is no vibration in it, nor any flowing. It does not consume oxygen, it does not divide, it does not grow, nor does it move.

All of life, even the experiments that have come close to developing life in a test tube have one thing in common—movement, if manifested only as energy being used up or transferred. To maintain life and the intricacies of its processes, energy must be utilized. The smallest, most primitive cell at rest or even dying, when placed in a scientific metabolic chamber, will continue to consume almost undetectable but still measurable amounts of oxygen. But a virus placed in the same chamber does nothing. There is no transfer of heat, no oxygen is used, no radiation given off or absorbed. For all practical purposes, outside the body it is dead, an inert polymer of DNA, lying within an inert protein sheath and so, since seemingly already dead, impossible to kill. . . .

Something happens to that [hepatitis] virus when it is reinjected into the body and re-enters liver cells. Oxygen suddenly begins to be consumed by the infected cell, heat is given off, energy is transferred and utilized as the virus comes gradually to life.

*   *   *

And so the confusion. Containing the polymer DNA, a chemical found only in living things, they seemed anything but alive; indeed, taken from the body and looked at under the microscope, they not only appeared but were absolutely inert. And yet they were obviously infective, able to multiply and cause disease when injected back into the human body.[6]

Getting off the Track: Descartes and Newton

We have all these new insights into how the pulsing of life is sustained. Yet despite our vision of these vast and intricate webs of connections among cells and tissues and organs, our modern popular view of ourselves and our world is still largely blind to the continuous quality of the web which constitutes life.

Why is this the case? The story is interesting and important. But at some points and to some readers it may seem complicated. To aid those who may wish for now to read only the highlights of this story and leave some of the actual detail for another day, the main body of the story will continue—marked in the margin by a thin border. Those who do wish to skip ahead will find the highlights printed in italics. What we are involved with here is nothing less than a new vision of ourselves and our connections to one another and our world.

Whether we are aware of it or not, our minds today are still drenched in assumptions from Newtonian science and its philosopher-progenitor, Rene Descartes. The physicist Fritjof Capra writes, "The birth of modern science was preceded and accompanied by a development of philosophical thought which led to an extreme formulation of the spirit/matter dualism. This formulation appeared in the seventeenth century in the philosophy of Rene Descartes who based his view of nature on a fundamental division into two separate and independent realms; that of mind (*res cogitans*), and that of matter (*res extensa*). The 'Cartesian' division allowed scientists to treat matter as dead and completely separate from themselves, and to see the material world as a multitude of different objects assembled into a huge machine."[7]

In its basic metaphors and ways of thinking about life, the popular view today is still based upon scientific views associated with the name of Sir Isaac Newton. Newtonian science was mechanistic: our bodies, brains and nature were likened to machines. It was also deterministic. Men had noticed in the world what seemed to be natural laws guiding cause and effect, so it seemed possible to observe with precision and thus learn to use those "laws." Newtonian science was also materialistic, and reality was thought to consist of empty space in which separate things— "matter"—moved. Object A moving through empty space would affect object B, which in turn did something to object C. And A, B and C could be either people or billiard balls or inclined planes; it made no difference. Capra writes:

As a consequence of the Cartesian division, most individuals are aware of themselves as isolated egos existing "inside" their bodies. . . . This inner fragmentation of man mirrors his view of the world "outside" which is seen as a multitude of separate objects and events.[8]

*When I now say that "We are interconnected," I do **not** use those terms within the thought world of Newtonian science. I do **not** mean just that there exist certain relationships between discrete entities, which bridge otherwise empty space. On the contrary, what I am meaning to convey when I am speaking of connections is the sense of a continuous reality so much of one piece as to make the whole notion of empty space and solid objects totally inappropriate.*

Beyond "Empty Space" and "Solid Objects"

In his book *The Tao of Physics* Fritjof Capra tells the fascinating story of how scientists in the early decades of this century discovered the limits of Newtonian thought. What they uncovered through their exploration of atoms and subatomic particles was a different sort of reality than we had previously even imagined.

[The laws of atomic physics] were not easy to recognize. They were discovered in the 1920s by an international group of physicists including Niels Bohr from Denmark, Louis De Broglie from France, Erwin Schroedinger and Wolfgang Pauli from Austria, Werner Heisenberg from Germany, and Paul Dirac from England. These men joined their forces across all national borders and shaped one of the most exciting periods in modern science, which brought man, for the first time, into contact with the strange and unexpected reality of the subatomic world.

Every time the physicists asked nature a question in an atomic experiment, nature answered with a paradox, and the more they tried to clarify the situation, the sharper the paradoxes became. It took them a long time to accept the fact that these paradoxes belong to the intrinsic structure of atomic physics, and to realize that they arise whenever one attempts to describe atomic events in the traditional terms of physics. Once this was perceived, the physicists began to learn to ask the right questions and to avoid contradictions. In the words of Heisenberg, "they somehow got into the spirit of the quantum theory," and finally they found the precise and consistent mathematical formulation of this theory.

The concepts of quantum theory were not easy to accept even after their mathematical formulation had been completed. Their effect on the physicists' imaginations was truly shattering. Rutherford's experiments had shown that atoms, instead of being hard and indestructible, consisted of vast regions of space in which extremely small particles moved, and now quantum theory made it clear that even *these particles were nothing like the solid objects of classical physics.* The subatomic units of matter are very abstract entities which have a dual aspect. Depending on how we look at them, they appear sometimes as particles, sometimes as waves; and this dual nature is also exhibited by light which can take the form of electromagnetic waves or of particles.

This property of matter and of light is very strange. It seems impossible to accept that something can be, at the same time, a particle—i.e., an entity confined to a very small volume—and a wave, which is spread out over a very large region of space.[9] (Emphasis added.)

*   *   *

The apparent contradiction between the particle and the wave picture was solved in a completely unexpected way which called in question the very foundation of the mechanistic world view—the concept of the reality of matter. At the subatomic level, matter does not exist with certainty at definite places, but rather shows "tendencies to exist," and atomic events do not occur with certainty at definite times and in definite ways, but rather show "tendencies to occur." In the formalism of quantum theory, these tendencies are expressed as probabilities and are associated with mathematical quantities which take the form of waves. This is why particles can be waves at the same time. They are not "real" three-dimensional waves like sound or water waves. They are "probability waves," abstract mathematical quantities with all the characteristic properties of waves which are related to the probabilities of finding the particles at particular points in space and at particular times. All the laws of atomic physics are expressed in terms of these probabilities. We can never predict an atomic event with certainty; we can only say how likely it is to happen.[10]

This twentieth-century discovery of a continuous and probablistic reality is totally foreign to us whose imaginations have been nourished within the world view of Newtonian science and within a political, social and intellectual life characterized by hierarchical orderings. Reality no longer has basic "building blocks." All that is put aside. A new metaphysic and philosophy of reality is suggested in which there are only dynamic webs of interconnections. Capra sets out the implications for us of this transformation of our understanding:

Quantum theory has thus demolished the classical concepts of solid objects and of strictly deterministic laws of nature. At the subatomic level, the solid material objects of classical physics dissolve into wave-like patterns of probabilities, and these patterns, ultimately, do not represent probabilities of things but rather *probabilities of interconnections.*[11] (Emphasis added.)

A Pervasive Dance of Energy

Relativity theory forced scientists to modify their concept of what a particle was if it wasn't a solid object, as we (and they) had grown up thinking:

> In classical physics, the mass of an object had always been associated with an indestructible material substance, with some "stuff" of which all things were thought to be made. *Relativity theory showed that mass has nothing to do with any substance, but is a form of energy.* Energy, however, is a dynamic quantity associated with activity, or with processes. The fact that the mass of a particle is equivalent to a certain amount of energy means that *the particle can no longer be seen as a static object, but has to be conceived as a dynamic pattern,* a process involving the energy which manifests itself as the particle's mass. . . .
>
> When two particles collide with high energies, they generally break into pieces, but these pieces are not smaller than the original particles. They are again particles of the same kind and are created out of the energy of motion ("kinetic energy") involved in the collision process. . . . This way, we can divide matter again and again, but we never obtain smaller pieces because we just create particles out of the energy involved in the process. The subatomic particles are thus destructible and indestructible at the same time.[12] (Emphasis added.)

So objects are not solid masses, as we have always thought. Objects are actually patterns of energy. This means that reality is not only more interconnected than we have imagined but also far more dynamic and creative:

> Quantum theory has shown that particles are not isolated grains of matter, but are probability patterns, interconnections in an inseparable cosmic web. Relativity theory, so to speak, has made these patterns come alive by *revealing their intrinsically dynamic character.* It has shown that the activity of matter is the very essence of its being. *The particles of the subatomic world are not only active in the sense of moving around very fast; they themselves are processes!* The existence of matter and its activity cannot be separated. They are but different aspects of the same space-time reality.[13] (Emphasis added.)

*   *   *

Subatomic particles are dynamic patterns which have a space aspect
and a time aspect. Their space aspect makes them appear as objects
with a certain mass, their time aspect as processes involving the
equivalent energy.

These dynamic patterns, or "energy bundles," form the stable
nuclear, atomic and molecular structures which build up matter and
give it its macroscopic solid aspect, thus making us believe that it is
made of some material substance. At the macroscopic level, this
notion of substance is a useful approximation, but at the atomic level
it no longer makes sense. *Atoms consist of particles and these
particles are not made of any material stuff. When we observe them,
we never see any substance; what we observe are dynamic patterns
continually changing into one another—a continuous dance of
energy.*[14] (Emphasis added.)

Western theology and philosophy have not come close to dealing
with such a dynamic reality. Only process philosophy in the
tradition of Alfred North Whitehead and the still-young process
theology begin to think about reality in such dynamic and wholistic
terms. Such dynamism and wholism break up the concepts of both
classical science and traditional philosophy and religion.

The Shattering of Old Concepts

Our popular ways of thinking about space and time and matter
have been undercut by modern physicists, as Capra explains:

Einstein's theory...says that *three-dimensional space is actually
curved*, and that the curvature is caused by the gravitational field of
massive bodies. Wherever there is a massive object, e.g., a star or a
planet, the space around it is curved and the degree of curvature
depends on the mass of the object. And as space can never be
separated from time in relativity theory, *time as well* is affected by the
presence of matter, *flowing at different rates in different parts of the
universe. Einstein's general theory of relativity thus completely
abolishes the concepts of absolute space and time.* Not only are all
measurements involving space and time relative; the whole structure
of space-time depends on the distribution of matter in the universe,
and the concept of "empty space" loses its meaning.[15] (Emphasis
added.)

All of this raises the serious question of whether our accustomed
thinking is adequate to the task of comprehending such a dynamic,
interconnected, but relative reality. Capra as a physicist puts the
problem this way:

Rational knowledge is thus a system of abstract concepts and symbols, characterized by the linear, sequential structure which is typical of our thinking and speaking. In most languages this linear structure is made explicit by the use of alphabets which serve to communicate experience and thought in long lines of letters.

The natural world, on the other hand, is one of infinite varieties and complexities, a multidimensional world which contains no straight lines or completely regular shapes, where things do not happen in sequences, but all together; a world where—as modern physics tells us—even empty space is curved. It is clear that our abstract system of conceptual thinking can never describe or understand this reality completely. In thinking about the world we are faced with the same kind of problem as the cartographer who tries to cover the curved face of the Earth with a sequence of plane [flat] maps. We can only expect an approximate representation of reality from such a procedure, and all rational knowledge is therefore necessarily limited.[16] (Emphasis added.)

The key which will open the door to the understanding of this vision of the universe cannot be our old key taken from Newtonian science. Those linear categories fit neither wholeness nor the dynamism of curved space and relative time. The key to such understanding of the universe will come from something other than our inadequate mental models and mental categories from the past.

*   *   *

I went out walking, intending to feel the world, not to think it. I tried to feel with that totally nonphysical sense—that unspeakable sense of unity which communes without absorbing, allies without possessing, perceives without categorizing.

It was snowing, but I didn't call it snow; I called it quiet. Wind swayed the grass fields, but I didn't call it grass; I called it rhythm. I sat on a stump and it became strength and companionship, rather than a hunk of wood.

And suddenly I was no separate matter-body thinking about these things; I was an integral part of their music, their heart-beat. I was helping to make the balance....

Slowly I'm burning the boxes and pigeon holes I've built up within infinity.

The music of a bird just touched my ears. I feel no need to identify the species. Someday I may not even need to name the singer "bird."[17]

No Place Apart

Quantum theory and Relativity theory make it clear that when we are talking about nature, we are not talking about something which is *apart* from us. Fritjof Capra writes:

> As we penetrate into matter, nature does not show us any isolated "basic building blocks," but rather appears as a complicated web of relations between the various parts of the whole. *These relations always include the observer in an essential way.* The human observer constitutes the final link in the chain of observational processes, and the properties of any atomic object can only be understood in terms of the object's interaction with the observer.[18] (Emphasis added.)

"This means," writes Capra, *"that the classical ideal of an objective description of nature is no longer valid. The Cartesian partition between [the] I and the world, between the observer and the observed, cannot be made when dealing with atomic matter. In atomic physics, we can never speak about nature without, at the same time, speaking about ourselves."*[19] (Emphasis added.)

What a challenge to traditional thinking and experiencing! What has disappeared—it was an illusion—is the partition of objectivity, the partition which in classical science was thought to separate the observer from what was being observed or done to.

What must also disappear—for it too is an illusion—is the partition which in the male attitude has been thought to separate males from that which in patriarchal society has been mythed as Other—woman, nature, things. Man has wanted to see himself as the creator and experiencer of history and culture—set apart from objects (lesser men, women, slaves, nature, things) which he could act upon, observe, and manipulate with detachment as though "above" and "apart." What I am saying is that reality is not Cartesian. It is not partitioned. It is not hierarchical. It does not consist of builders and building-blocks, observers and observed, doers and done-to. Reality is a complex and dynamic web of energy and relationships which simply includes the human, both female and male.

The implications of this for the Western mind are staggering, for we are the inheritors of a patriarchal tradition which goes back at least to Judaism. We are inheritors of a body/spirit dualism from the Greeks. And in our technology and our everyday understanding of science we are inheritors of the Cartesian categories. Furthermore, we have been nurtured in the problem-solving ways of scientific reductionism, which divides problems into component parts, splitting one thing from another ("The better to eat them, my dear!" as the Big Bad Wolf said to Little Red Riding Hood).

A Single Connected Wholeness

Whether we look into the science of the infinitely small (subatomic physics) or into the science of the human body and living cells (medicine and cell biology)—or, as we will do in the next chapter, into the science of ecology and the global life-supporting web of the biosphere and its ecosystems—what you will find is a single connected wholeness. Everything is immediately or remotely affecting and being affected by everything else. The religious mystic in a seventh heaven of revelation, or nighttime swimmers sharing the ecstasy of water, sky, stars—all have intensely personal intimations of a truth we are now coming to know: our world at the core of its being is everywhere connected.

8.

Distracted by Conflict
from Seeing Whole

The freshness of the early morning is magical. The gulls are almost quiet, and the sea has a soft velvety quality to it. It is so still this morning that the boat hulls have reflections below them, which almost never happens. Everything smells moist after the hard rain last night. The soft morning light strikes the pencil-thin shapes of boat masts and makes them gleam all out of proportion to their slim dimensions. A very light wind slowly ripples the reflections toward me, while some early-bird gulls swoop low for their breakfast. The whole area seems to be bathed in promise, in the implicit coming-to-be of a new day. Everything is holding its breath, waiting. One of our cats goes out to stalk in the high sea-grass. A small duck family, one behind the other, sculls along on the quiet water without causing a ripple. I hear vague waking sounds from the cottage next door. The wind picks up and streaks water once velvety-similar into triangular patches of lighter and darker water. There on the horizon the first sailboat, and over there the first motor boat. The day begins.

Why Our Preoccupation with "Difference" and "Conflict"?

If we experience each moment in the wholeness of our senses, then why have we been more intent upon the parts of what we saw than upon their coordination? More intent upon conflict in what we were seeing than upon symbiosis? Even a cursory look at our recent past suggests a number of reasons for our distraction.

It is clear that we have been distracted by the surface phenomena. We've been very intent upon who is eating whom and who has been winning and losing. It has been easy to miss the dependence of the predator species upon the species which is its prey.

It is also apparent that we have looked at our world with hierarchical glasses on. We have seen things structured as those glasses prepared us to see them. Consequently everything seemed structured in hierarchies of one sort or another—hierarchies of status, or power, or logical priority, or even temporal sequence. Hence we rated species as well as individuals and social classes as "above" or "below" in terms of complexity, accomplishments, rationality, evolutionary place, or even who was "higher" on the food chain of who was eating whom.

Finally, we have also taken themes of social conflict from the currents of thought in a particular historical epoch and then projected (or "found") those themes of conflict in nature too. Loren Eiseley, writing in *Darwin's Century*, tells how "England, in the first phase of the Industrial Revolution and frightened by the excesses of the French monarchial overthrow, [took] readily to the bleak expression of the human struggle as portrayed by Malthus. The doctrine of the survival of the fittest would lie ready to the hand of Darwin."[1] So men who had grown up seeing all around them the harsh competitiveness and struggle of the working classes to survive amid the excesses of early industrialization then looked at nature and saw it "raw in tooth and claw" and shaped by "the survival of the fittest." Conflict and competition among species for food and niches do exist. But we err if that is all we perceive.

Some reputable scientists today look at nature and see coordination and symbiosis as more fundamental than conflict. In his book *The Lives of a Cell* the biologist Lewis Thomas reflects about what he sees to be a very basic force or tendency "for living things to join up, establish linkages, live inside each other, return to earlier arrangements, get along, whenever possible."[2]

> If this is, in fact, the drift of things, the way of the world, we may come to view immune reactions, genes for the marking of self, *and perhaps all reflexive responses of aggression and defense as secondary developments in evolution, necessary for the regulation and modulation of symbiosis, not designed to break into the process, only to keep it from getting out of hand.*[3] (Emphasis added.)

In another section Lewis Thomas points to what he calls the simplest and most spectacular symbol of this tendency—the phenomenon of cell fusion:

> In a way it is the most unbiologic of phenomena, violating the most fundamental myth of the last century, for it denies the importance of the specificity, integrity, and separateness in living things. Any cell— man, animal, fish, fowl, or insect—given the chance and under the right conditions, brought into contact with any other cell, however foreign, will fuse with it. Cytoplasm will flow easily from one to the

other, the nuclei will combine, and it will become, for a time anyway, a single cell with two complete, alien genomes, ready to dance, ready to multiply.[4]

Thus in cell biology as well as in subatomic physics the forward edge of discovery and thought are leading to ways of thinking about life and reality which deny our inherited ways of seeing the world as separate entities moving in empty space. It now appears we need to look at our world with new eyes which can see more.

Ecology as a New Way of Seeing

Abner Dean has drawn a cartoon showing a roomful of people at a cocktail party. At first glance the gathering appears normal; some are standing, some sitting, all are holding drinks and deep in conversations. But then you realize that some of the arms are greatly elongated and extend like spaghetti out around people so as to hold hands with other people across the room. The caption reads: "You have to know how to look at a roomful of people."

Exactly! You also have to know how to look at the created world. We have not perceived the connections—the hand-holding and exchanges of benefits among species which also compete—in short, the extent of symbiotic relations which have been in nature all along.

Ecology is the scientific discipline which has finally become a lens for seeing and describing the connections in the biosphere. What ecology helps us see is an earth covered with a vast array of ecosystems, both large and small, continuously interacting with one another in many ways which are not immediately obvious to humans.

There are, in addition to the more localized ecosystems, the vast biospheral life-supporting systems. These are the recycling systems of the land, air and water. They are all powered by the energy of the sun and continually providing energy and food for countless ecosystems even while reprocessing their wastes. Another generation looked at clouds becoming rain and snow, which became glaciers and rivers and oceans, which in turn evaporated to become clouds again—and saw in this the conflict of heat and cold and the conflict of seasons. But as this great hydrological cycle works, all that dwells upon the earth is watered and sustained in life. Similarly, the attention of earlier generations has been more caught by the fact that animals *ate* plants, and they have not been very aware that plants also give out oxygen which animals breathe in, and that in turn the animals breathe out carbon dioxide and provide nutrients in the form of manure which plants need to take in. Photosynthesis in the plants uses solar energy to convert that carbon dioxide and those nutrients into carbohydrates—the beginning of all food eaten by animals, humans, fish, reptiles, birds, or insects. And everything which eats (or is eaten) finally dies and decays and becomes in turn fertile compost for future plant-growth and photosynthesis.

Yes, there is conflict and competition. But it is all within ecosystems and biospheral systems which connect life with life.

The Flies, the Geckos, and the Cats

The first principle of ecology is wholism—that everything is connected directly or indirectly and affects everything else. Nothing operates in isolation. One biologist tells this story to illustrate the point.

> Some years ago the World Health Organization launched a mosquito control program in Borneo and sprayed large quantities of DDT, which had proved to be a very effective means in controlling the mosquito. But, shortly thereafter, the roofs of the natives' houses began to fall because they were being eaten by caterpillars, which, because of their particular habits, had not absorbed very much of the DDT themselves. A certain predatory wasp, however, which had been keeping the caterpillars under control, had been killed off in large numbers by the DDT. But the story does not end there, because they brought the spraying indoors to control houseflies. Up to that time, the control of houseflies was largely the job of the little lizard, the gecko, that inhabits houses. Well, the geckos continued their job of eating flies, now heavily dosed with DDT, and the geckos began to die. Then the geckos were eaten by house cats. The poor house cats at the end of this food chain had concentrated this material and they began to die. And they died in such numbers that rats began to invade the houses and consume the food. But more important, the rats were potential plague carriers. This situation became so alarming that they finally resorted to parachuting fresh cats into Borneo to try to restore the balance of populations that the people, trigger-happy with the spray guns, had destroyed.[5]

"Everything Is Connected"

On a global scale these same interconnections are evident from the fact that DDT (as well as PCBs and radioactive nuclides) have been found in the tissues of all organisms tested to date. These substances have been found in the flesh of the flightless penguins of the Antarctic even though these substances have never been introduced by human activities onto the Antarctic continent. These substances have been obtained by the penguins through a series of food chains leading to the oceans and thus extending outside the Antarctic.

As we see from these examples, chemical substances cycle through and among ecosystems by various paths and at various rates. Energy also passes through these ecosystems following a one-way downhill path, sometimes circuitous but always being dissipated eventually as heat, and never returning to its former usefulness. We are coming to perceive that what we as humans do takes place amid these ongoing processes.

It is this continual flow of energy through ecosystem paths which Eleanor and Clifford West sense as they describe lovely Ossabaw Island on Georgia's Atlantic coastline:

> Waters from the rivers,
>   from the place itself
>   and from the ocean
> feed the marshland's generators of energy—
>   sun-drenched and wind blown—
> and link the strong but tenuous food chains
>   and channels of energy which flow,
>   cycle and recycle in powerful but delicate systems,
> ancient as the world,
>   present as a cresting wave,
> but with a malleable future.[6]

Diversity and Interdependence

Not only are we interconnected in ways we have not understood; life is also coordinated and symbiotic. We have been blinded to this by our patterns of male competitiveness and by our notions of "survival of the fittest."

Diversity and interdependence are motifs in creation which weave together like a Bach fugue. You cannot understand the one without the other. Yes, there is conflict. Yes, there is competition. But we need to readjust our mental models or paradigms so we are able also to perceive coordination in all these systems as more fundamental than conflict. We must put aside our mental filters which let us see nothing but conflict and competition. We must see the world as it is—powerfully diverse and full of conflict as well as powerfully interdependent.

Different Roles in the Dance of Life

The ordering in such an interconnected and interdependent reality is functional—rather than hierarchical. None are really above or below. Each has a role to play in the dance of life.

A symbol springs to mind. Picture several dancers holding hands, whirling in space and leaning backward against the tension of those clasped hands. It would be immediately obvious looking at them that no one of them is more important than the others; that they mutually hold one another in position; and that if one of them were to move in such a way as to cause another to fall, the support upon which each depends would be gone.

We are one of those dancers within the dance of life. But we are mutually held in position by every other species, by the rain and sun and the vast unseen food chains and recycling systems, even down to the smallest phytoplankton in the oceans. We mutually support one another in the interconnections which flow through our bodies and life-histories.

We Are within—Not apart from—the Dance of Life

We err if we think of ourselves as separate from this dance of life, or above it. We are inextricably and irreversibly within it. But in our vast anthropocentric pretension we are now destroying the other dancers, oblivious to the "rhythm that is greater than our own."[7]

In a system everything affects—and is affected by—everything else. On the other hand, in a hierarchy those on top—those with power—affect those below. And those below do not talk back! But secretaries *do* affect their bosses's behavior; sergeants and lieutenants and privates *do* limit what generals and colonels can attempt; the Borneo house cat at the "top" of the food chain *is* affected by the diet of the gecko lizard and the exposure to DDT of the houseflies.

The ordering within hierarchical systems perceives only who gives the orders and who takes them. It is an ordering based upon a chain of command and upon a simple, straight-line and one-way understanding of causality. Such thinking is linear thinking and when taken literally as a description of how a whole system is organized or ordered, it is incomplete and misleading. Inevitably those lines of command generate effects which come back to affect whatever is at their starting point. Those who are "above" in hierarchical systems frequently underestimate the extent of their own self-interest in the well-being of those "below."

Self-Interest's Boomerang

Malthus and Darwin led us off the track with their emphasis upon ruthless competition. We have misread the biosphere and the energy-dance of life. Similarly in the human realm we have been led off the track by understanding human relations in dog-eat-dog terms. If every relationship were one in which someone won and someone else lost, then clearly your own self-interest would lie in winning as much of the time as you could. But seeing the world that way assumes a Newtonian separate-bodies-in-empty-space view of things. It misses completely the systemic and interrelated character of life in human society. It is insensitive to what I call self-interest's boomerang.

Self-interest is one of the ways we focus upon what is good for one part of a system, rather than upon what is good for the whole. Self-interest which stops at your own skin is an expression of the (erroneous) conviction that you can do a good thing for yourself even if you diminish another part of the system, or even diminish the whole system.

The illusion is that the "I-win" part of a social system can be disconnected from the "You-lose" part. This assumes there is an "away" to throw our social problems to. Or, conversely, that there is some "away" winners can retreat to, such as to the suburbs or to high-security high-rise urban apartment buildings, escaping all the losers who somehow still hang onto life and hang onto the anger they have learned.

But human society in its vastness, its diversity, and its complexity, has many of the system-characteristics of the simple boomerang: what is cast "away" returns after a little time from a somewhat different direction. In social systems the result is frequent irony. Consider, for example, the principal figures in Watergate who were tried in Washington, D.C., before largely black juries on conspiracy charges. These were the same men who had devised and implemented for President Nixon his so-called Southern Strategy for winning the 1968 election and who later, in order to deal with Vietnam War protesters, had sought enactment of that conspiracy legislation.

Or consider New England's present-day struggle to pay for its swollen welfare rolls. New England's industrialization in the early 1800s had been financed in substantial part by profits from New England ships engaged in the Triangle Trade, taking trinkets, rum and slaves between New England, Africa and Southern ports. New England struggles now to pay those delayed bills as it receives back to the welfare rolls, along with many who are white or Hispanic, many also who are descendents of slaves who had originally been sold to the Old South.

Again, ghetto youth had been ravaged by drugs in the 1940s and 1950s while a white power structure in our cities concentrated on other urban problems. Many whites felt they could get away from drug-related problems by living in white suburbs. Not until white youth in the suburbs and in the colleges began using those same drugs in quantity did drugs become a priority problem. And in my experience, those who complain about law-and-order and feel abused because they cannot walk the streets safely at night, do not seem to understand that they themselves laid the fundations for this crime and violence when they tolerated social and economic arrangements which do not provide for all people work and dignity and a stake in the established order.

The feedback loops in our interconnected social systems are as tangible as those in our natural ecosystems. We have just not had eyes to see them. Many still think they can get "away" from those who have been hurt and made angry in the competition and "survival of the fittest" legitimated by our social Darwinism. They think they will have, as their forebears did, some place to go to for a new start—a "West" to move on to after you have depleted the goodwill and nutrients of the "soil" you have grown in and depended upon.

The Whole-System Ethic

Cartoonist Stan Hunt helps us laugh about the futility of such attempts to get away while still depending upon a very interconnected and interdependent society. Hunt shows us people perched around the perimeter of a rubber lifeboat bobbing on the waves far out in the ocean, and one of the people is saying to the others, "Pardon me, but your end of the lifeboat is sinking."

What we need is a whole-system ethic which identifies the absurdity of a doctrine of self-interest which ends at our own skin and does not help us see beyond the immediate present to the larger contexts upon which we depend for life and of which we are a part.

An ethic which looks at whole-systems certainly begins by examining systematically in decision after decision such questions as: Who *gains* from this or that? . . . who profits? And does anyone *lose* by this or that? . . . the poor? . . . the earth? . . . generations yet to come? Some costs are inherently unknowable now, and must be allowed for, because they become payable if there are future surprises (and experience tells us there often are). Such questions are particularly important when those deciding (or benefiting) are different from those who will in one way or another be asked to pay the bill. When we ourselves must pay, we take care to ask ourselves about the costs; we must be equally careful or perhaps more so when others (whom we are connected with and affected by) will pay.

Choices framed in win/lose terms pose a special problem for an ethic sensitive to connections within a system. When armed with a systemic ethic, one can make a good case for avoiding and rejecting the terms of all choices which are win/lose choices, whether the system is your body, your marriage or family, or the nations of the world, or some other system. Even where effects are delayed (as when post-dated checks come due much later) or where effects are displaced (so someone else has to pay the bill), such win/lose arrangements are utterly destructive of system morale and harmony. The system solidarity of family life is diminished by resentments. Individual morale is eroded by illness or other system-impairments. So too, trust among groups, nations, and generations is drained away by persistent imbalances in the terms by which benefits, costs and risks are exchanged.

The all-win character of whole-system ethics has often seemed difficult and impractical when viewed from positions of some security, privilege and power. But nations, like individuals, sometimes learn from experience. After World War I the winning Allies had extracted reparations from the losers in that war. The seeds of starvation and despair were sown in post-war Germany, and we reaped the whirlwind in the rise of Hitler and Nazism. Following World War II there were those among the leaders of the winning Allies who felt they had learned a lesson from history. Instead of beating down the losers by again extracting reparations, we chose to pour money into the countries we had just defeated in what came to be called The Marshall Plan. A judgment had been made somewhere that our common welfare was going to be only as good as the postwar welfare of the losers in that conflict.

The Case of the Big Apple

New York City's continuing financial crises provide an interesting example of our vacillations between win/lose and all-win policies, and of our still-dawning awareness of interconnections.

When the bankruptcy of New York City was perceived, midway through President Ford's administration, to mean only the fall of one spendthrift city which had too many poor and too many social services for its income, the then-powers-that-be in Washington and Wall Street were willing to see the Big Apple punished like a wayward daughter. New York City was to be an example to others who might be tempted to similar financial behavior. But then it began to become apparent that if New York City went down the drain of financial bankruptcy, then it would take with it the marketability of municipal bonds for all cities and also the profitability of many major U.S. banks (which had been heavily invested in tax-exempt municipal bonds). In short, "default" on its bonds by New York would have had ripple effects not only in national but in global systems of banking and trade. As all this became more clear over several weeks and months, it suddenly appeared to many who have a say in such matters that the price of "punishing" and making an example of New York City was too high. Whether we had realized it or not (and whether we liked it or not), we were connected by heretofore unperceived threads to the Big Apple and its swollen budgets and urban poor.

The City of New York worked diligently in subsequent months to make its suppliers across the country aware of the implications of the City not paying its bills or the City stopping further orders. Suppliers (as well as their employees and Congressional representatives and the rest of us) suddenly learned much more specifically how what happens to New York City affects profits, jobs, and communities far away.

Enlarging the Scope of Our Self-Interest

Our interdependence is so complex that we may well conclude it is foolish to destroy *any* part of what we depend upon but do not fully understand. That is the point of the all-win ethic: we need to refuse as inadequate and probably too simple those alternatives which are presented to us in win/lose terms. We are supported by many invisible threads which connect us to other dancers in the dance of life, and some of these dancers and these threads we are not even aware of. It is only at our own peril that we destroy them.

In such a world it is no longer simply altruistic or religious to "Love your neighbors" or, as Jesus counseled, to "Love your enemies." This perception of our world and its web of connections so enlarges the scope of our self-interest that, as Hazel Henderson has observed, "For the first time in history, morality has become pragmatic."[8]

9.

Lost Dimensions
of Human Identity

I must stop periodically as I write to go to the basement to bring up laundry from the washing machine. We have just had a houseful of guests and there are mounds of sheets and towels to be washed and spread out to dry on the deck beside me. It is a magnificent drying day, overflowing with sun which warms the laundry and with wind which billows it out in great puffs of drying contour sheets. The sun is glinting on the always-moving waves in millions of sparkles. The energy dance. As the sheets and towels dry, they are filled with the good smells of fresh sun and wind, and as I fold them I bury my face in their goodness again and again. As I work, my body and spirit seem fed with the goodness of those natural elements. Why have we separated ourselves from all the sun and wind have to give us? Why have we dried our clothes in technological boxes and then dreamed up chemical fragrances to give (as the ad says) "that fresh smell of clothes dried out-of-doors"? Why do we prefer foods chemically processed to the food as it was naturally? Why have we preferred our technological marvels over and over again?

My spirit thrives here by the shore in the summer, where the activities of our days must be in cooperation with what the wind and sun and rain and water are doing. When the sun is shining, you work in the sun or swim or contemplate the wonder of creation. When the day is overcast or rainy, you do indoor things such as iron, read by the fire, or go to town to the stores. And every day you scan the sky and clouds for a sense of what will be coming next. My spirit is nurtured by such dialogue; my days are shaped and enriched by the limitations of what is possible.

But come September when we go back to our other life, we return to a life largely inside. It is work-oriented and nothing we do is determined by the weather. The sterile sameness of days walled away from my summer dialogue with sun and wind and weather gets to me. I am eroded, thinned, flattened in spirit. No one we work with seems aware. Dining at the faculty club, no one notices. They turn from windswept river and magnificent skyline view to one another's words and ordering lunch. Is it that they have never lived enough with the out-of-doors or with the sea? All of which leads me to ask, Do we know who we really are as humans? Or are we but a shadow of our true selves, getting by with a diminished sense of our human identity given us along with our history, the language we use to think and speak, and the social functions or roles which occupy our time?

Alienation in Myth and Identity

I am struck by a line from *Manas:* "The myth supplies the materials for self-identification. This is its primary function."[1] In that event our hierarchical myths of Western civilization, scientific as well as religious, have served us badly. They have provided us with a sense of ourselves which, like Humpty Dumpty fallen off the wall, is "in pieces." Our inherited sense of self is deeply split and dualistic, and in science, in philosophy, in psychology, in theology, we are laboriously trying to glue the pieces back together in order to understand what it is to be human.

Our old myths from both science and religion have told us we were split and apart, spirit (or mind) apart from our physical bodies and flesh. Ernest Becker's phrase about our being "gods with anuses" was a striking way to express this dominant theme of self-understanding in Western thought.

Pain and the Awareness of Wholeness

My own personal story is a study in the inadequacy of our split-apart self-concept. I was well-trained by long years of college and graduate professional school to enjoy the male world of intellectual activities and initiative-taking, and therefore I viewed myself as males are trained to do—as almost exclusively mind and will. That was who I was. My selfhood transcended my body and had no important reference to my body. My body was merely what allowed me to act out my mind and will.

How do I tell you about my rebirth of identity as I discovered my selfhood in relation to my body? I was sick for a two-month period, bed-ridden with pneumonia and a severe relapse. I discovered within the limiting six surfaces of that one room how my world view was constricted by the weakness of my body. Mind and will were limited by body. Some years later I had a soul-searing brush with death, fearing I had breast cancer. You discover then—and not just in the clearly held convictions at the surface of your mind but deep in your gut—that *you are mortal.* And you know a loneliness and fear which belongs to being a woman with a woman's breasts. Still again, I was pregnant several times with our children. In pregnancy and childbirth you find experiences which are if not soul-searing then soul-changing, because again your body is a woman's body, not a man's.

In all these experiences you discover that *all of you* is in that body. Your mind and your will and everything that there has ever been or ever will be of you is "in" and "expressed through" and "experiencing" with that woman's body that is your own. That body *is* your self. And you gradually realize, even while you grow in love with your husband, that no matter how equal to him you are and no matter how sympatique he is with you, he still cannot go through those physical experiences that you do. He is different, a man. He is different; his is not only another body but it is a different body, a man's body.

I heard later of theologian H. Richard Niebuhr's reaction to his brother Reinhold's stroke, and I realized that our experiences and moral reflections were akin at this point. Seeing his brother, so thoughtful and dynamic and creative—yet now encased and imprisoned by the limitations of his paralyzed flesh, Richard Niebuhr is reported to have found here a new appreciation for the incarnated quality of the human spirit: how enfleshed in a particular body the You that is yourself actually is. Niebuhr would characterize this as responding to God limiting us—reminding us of our mortal, created existence in which "all flesh is grass."

In my own case it gradually dawned upon me that any self-concept I might have of myself was seriously lacking if it did not take sufficient account of my body and its experiences of its own mortality in pleasure and in pain. I must now always include my body whenever I think of myself. I must now shape a self-concept which has a woman's bodily form.

Integrating the Inner Pieces of Our Selfhood

What seems to be emerging in our time is a healing of the old dualisms which divided mind from body, spirit from flesh. This new sense of wholeness in our identity is expressed succinctly by Penelope Washbourn when she says "*I am* my body,"[2] and by the title the Boston Women's Health Cooperative gave their first book: *Our Bodies, Ourselves.*

I think it was probably our dawning awareness of the psychosomatic nature of illness and healing that started us toward thinking whole about ourselves. Biofeedback and other clues to the psychosomatic nature of healing are reinforcing this whole direction of thought.[3] "There are a growing number of facts available," writes Ronald Glasser in *The Body Is the Hero,* "that show plainly we are as much a part of our own diseases as we are of our health, that we should be able to and indeed can help ourselves."[4]

Biospiritual Organisms

So the first and most basic step to a rebirth of an integrated inner identity is to realize that we are what theologian Kenneth Cauthen has called *"biospiritual organisms."* But we are not alone in having this sort of identity. This is equally true of all matter, whether a rock or a tree or a dolphin or chimp.

Life comes "all together." The problem is in our minds, in our concepts of ourselves, for the basis of all life, both physical and psychic, is unified in what we have been calling "the dance of energy." Body, mind, spirit, matter—these are all abstractions, metaphors which have socialized us to see and understand ourselves "in pieces." The efforts today of philosophers, psychologists and theologians to glue back together those pieces seem absurd in the light of the unity we now know is the basis of existence.

Perhaps as process theologians such as Cauthen have been suggesting, God too is a biospiritual unity just as all life in God's creation has a biospiritual character. *Perhaps there never is spirit without body and no body (or mass) without spirit.* Is it in this sense that we are created in God's image? Have we put asunder what God created joined together? We now struggle like children to glue together the broken chards of our erroneous metaphors!

As a part of this integration process, we must struggle also to glue together again our feeling and our thinking. Feeling has been so downgraded in our culture (as "feminine") and thinking (since it was declared masculine) so elevated into clouds of abstraction, that it is difficult to recall that humans have a thought every time we have a feeling and a feeling with every thought. Thinking and feeling are contiguous human processes constantly interpenetrating one another as we experience our lives. It is only as we repress each in turn that it comes to seem we have the one without the other. It is rare in Western culture that we acknowledge both as present at once, as for example Rene Dubos has done in this introduction to a lecture about "The Theology of the Earth":

> My presentation will be a mixture of the emotional response of my total being to the beauty of the earth, and of my mental processes as a scientist trying to give a rational account of the earth's association with living things. The phrase "theology of the earth" thus denotes for me the scientific understanding of the sacred relationships that link mankind to all the physical and living attributes of the earth.[5]

Embracing Our Collective Identity as Humans

Even if one living human being manages to glue together—or even fuse together—a wholistic sense of self, we will have only begun the task of forging a wholistic identity for all of us as humans. For we keep wanting to think about "nature" as "out there" somehow apart from "us" "in here." Many people who care about the environment still see it as outside of humans—as "those trees and hills and mountains."

But we who are within the energy dance are participants. *The cosmic dance of energy moves in us as it does in everything else,* and to believe still in the solidity of discrete entities such as our bodies or the mountains is simply not to understand either reality or who we ourselves are. "The stars and the seas," Kenneth Cauthen writes, "the earth and the earthworm, are not simply outside us as strangers. They are also with us as *participants in the adventure.* The elements in our tissues, the salt content of our blood, the rhythms of waking and sleeping, and the chemical processes in our brains all unite us to the whole web of life and matter evolving throughout the immensities of time and space."[6]

We said all that earlier in chapter 7 and 8. The point here, however, is that we have not yet incorporated that *reality of who we are* into our self-concept—our understanding of ourselves as human.

At Home Again upon the Earth

Who-we-are is rooted in our kinship with the natural. The water of life flows through our tissues, and we are nourished, watered, fed, sustained, and ultimately return everything in our bodies to the world around us.

Yet today we have lost this sense of kinship with the earth which in other generations told us where we came from and whither we finally go: "Dust thou art, and to dust thou shalt return." We are like cut-flowers living in glass vases. We have forgotten and often deny our dependence upon our roots in the biospheral systems of the earth. Unthinkingly and uncaring, we "do in" species near us and forget our need—and the globe's need—of them. Alienated from our natural setting, we busily put up more glass buildings and cover more of the land with pavement, thus isolating ourselves still further. Enclosed in buildings, we cut ourselves off from any awareness of our need for the overarching sky, the sun, the rain, the wind, the snow. *The conclusion is inescapable: we do not understand who we are.*

The consequences of our too-small self-concept is vividly described by the psychoanalyst Allen Wheelis as "not knowing how to live."

> Not knowing how to live is separateness, the division of the world into self and others. I sit inside my skull and look out as a frightened man from a moated castle. Me in here and the world out there. We negotiate, we make deals, exchanges, but we are not one. I am an entity, complete. Never do I lose sight of where I stop and the world begins. With sleepless vigilance I patrol the edges of selfhood, warn visitors away. I am independent within this domain, but am dying. It is my wholeness that destroys me. I long for partness in a greater whole. Knowing how to live is oneness with the world. I die of the hunger of oneness.[7]

Like Kunte Kinte in Alex Haley's *Roots*, we only know who we are as we appropriate to ourselves our kinship with the earth, which tells us where we have come from and provides the backdrop for understanding who-we-are, our dignity and destiny. We are like adopted children, adopted by the human culture within which we have been raised. Until we come to grips with the mysterious presence in us of the gifts and heritage of the good earth and rain and sun and stars, we will not understand all that we are and all that we are becoming.

Larger Identity Means Larger Self-Interest

Knowing what we are a part of, give to, and take from, gives to us a larger sense of self-interest. It softens the margins of a personal identity, a single body, and any one moment in time. so that we know we live for more than what may be good for *this* moment or pleasurable for *my* body or profitable *for me*. Those concerns do not disappear. But they find their fulfillment within a larger setting.

This larger setting includes all the other humans and species and times and places I clearly or dimly perceive to be tied in with the significance of my own living.

We will have an environmental ethic when self-interest becomes inclusive, when we sense that what hurts any part of my larger system will hurt me. The Sioux Indian proverb—"With all beings and all things we shall be as relatives"[8] sums up this larger identity of each of us with the wholeness we contribute to and receive from. Some day, perhaps we shall have an identity that can enjoy the earth as friend, provider and home. When that happens, we will know that when the earth hurts, it will hurt us. Then the environmental ethic will not just be in our heads but in our hearts—in the nerve endings of our sensitivity.

This is what it means to be at home again upon the earth. About this sense of life and home Ian McHarg writes:

> From the ecological view one can see that, since life is only transmitted by life, then, by living, each one of us is physically linked to the origins of life and thus—literally, not metaphorically—to all life. Moreover, since life originated from matter then, by living, man is physically united back through the evolution of matter to the primeval hydrogen. The planet Earth has been the one home for all of its processes and all of its myriad inhabitants since the beginning of time, from hydrogen to men. Only the bathing sunlight changes. Our phenomenal world contains our origins, our history, our milieu; it is our home.[9]

Perhaps, in these days, one has to have a special place on the planet to be aware of the power of this larger context of earth-home to nurture in us a larger sense of self. Ossabaw Island in Georgia has been such a place for many artists and creative people. Lin Root writes about this.

> Ossabaw provides the privilege of solitude; *the comfort of kinship;* a deep response to the strange power of the island; and more, *much more that nourishes the spirit and makes it fruitful.* Just as the fantastic flora of Ossabaw put forth roots and shoots, and multiply, so the writers, painters, sculptors, composers, scientists, scholars, project members of every type *find their work taking on new dimensions,* expanding in unforeseen directions. This is certainly the way in which the island has affected my work. Trying to analyze the many gifts I have received from Ossabaw—*I have come to realize that the gift of highest value—is the gift of self. Ossabaw allows me to become more truly my own person.*[10] (Emphasis added.)

10.

A New View of the Body

The sea is in an incredible boil this afternoon. The sun is still shining warmly.But the breeze which earlier sped countless sailboats across the open horizon has turned into a giant phantom hand which is slapping the water into pounding surfing waves. The air is punctuated with the excited screams of children body-surfing and with the powerful slaps of the surf on the beach. Whitecaps streak the water off the outer islands, and in our cove white water cascades down the beach and over the rocks on either side. I am reminded of the complexity of the waves at Point Lobos as I watch the waves work on the outer rocks. The foam spray shoots up into the air from one wave just as another dark wave crests behind it. Now the entire beach is white with one long wave which looms like a white cliff and then falls, subsiding into a froth of boiling, bubbling, eddying foam. Our son is cresting the waves on a surfboard while the sailboats at their moorings wobble crazily back and forth on the swells. For a while each wave seems higher than the last, and the spray now shoots over the outer rocks in tall fountains of airy cascading water. And from the breakers there rises stronger than usual the moist rich smell of the sea.

For our usually protected cove, it is a very special time. It is a wonderfully physical and vigorous afternoon which, like a strong lover, is full of contradictions. It is a vignette of California ocean transported to the Northeast. Its winds and waves are fit for storms but still the sun shines.

Psychic Celibacy

Eugene Bianchi is a former Jesuit priest and theologian who now teaches at a Protestant theological school. He writes of emerging from the cocoon of religious celibacy and makes this startling comment about the life of the secular male in today's culture:

For a long time I thought that celibacy was a prerogative unique to the Catholic clergy and nuns. Now I realize that celibacy is deeply rooted in our society at large.

Does this sound preposterous in the age of Hugh Hefner, the pill and permissiveness? Maybe it will help if I distinguish between physical and psychic celibacy. The physical celibate renounces sexual contact with the opposite sex or with another of one's own sex. Rules for Catholic religious professionals still insist on this kind of celibacy, although the post-Vatican Council II environment threatens old restrictions. *Psychic celibacy consists in keeping women mentally and affectionally at arm's length. It is in fact the core dogma of our patriarchal era.* Women can be exalted as wife, virgin, mother, or deprecated (and enjoyed) as temptress, playmate, whore. In whatever way this male projection works woman is object, nonequal, manipulated, *distanced.* Such a world is profoundly celibate.... Deliberation and decision at the top take place in a male lodge where the cultural myths of masculinity reign supreme.[1] (Emphasis added.)

*   *   *

Woman's place is one of enforced psychic celibacy. She is not encountered as a contributing equal to men in occupational and civic life.... On the level of mind and decision in the public sphere there is little or no intercourse between men and women. In this realm our performance and profit society is as celibate as a Trappist monastery. Unwritten but very real "Cloister" signs hang outside the board rooms, menacing excommunication (subtle and crass discriminations) for trespassing....

Women as wives, daughters, sisters, lovers are the working nuns of America; they clear a way and a time for their high priests to attend to sacred priorities. The woman widowed by weekend TV football is a symptom of the psychic celibacy syndrome. That many women refuse to recognize their situation is not surprising. Having internalized the system, they find derivative self-worth by imitation of the master class and enjoyment of material pacifiers.[2]

This ascetic aspect of the business ethos is not surprising. Max Weber, Ernst Troeltsch and R. H. Tawney (among others) have written about the role of ascetic Protestantism in the rise of capitalism: the heirs of Calvin, redirecting the sense of "calling" and the devotion and concern of the monasteries, worked in the world and in business with the same devotion and concern for proving they were God's elect and their immortal souls were saved. And on such a rigorous footrace for salvation, the body and sexuality must not distract one from the prize of salvation or success, which is strained toward with every breath of dedication. So when either Church or Corporation says, "You must put my demands before your family's," it does not seem strange. And when male business society is as cloistered psychically from women as a monastery, it does not seem strange. Such is the life of the ascetic. And once you have joined the race, coveted the prize, and internalized the rules, it does not seem strange at all.

From her research in historical theology the Roman Catholic theologian Rosemary Ruether supplies us with another piece of our jigsaw puzzle:

> In ascetic cultures, sex hardly disappears as a fact of life. But it must be debased into a depersonalized sphere where it can be make no spiritual demands. The body is objectified as an alien, dangerous force that must be crushed into submission. What this means is that the realm of bodily experience becomes separated out as a "lower realm" where one might capitulate to this force, but in a way that cannot be integrated into the moral and responsible self. Concubinage for the celibate priest and prostitution for the puritanical Victorians were the "underworld" created to compensate for the work of sublimated idealism.
>
> We must see that a power relationship of supra- and subordination between men and women is essential to this schism of mind and body. Only by making one person in the relationship inferior, dependent and "purely carnal," can one assure a sexuality without the challenge of interpersonalism. By making woman "carnal," one does not have to relate to her as a person. Asceticism does not have the effect of preventing the ascetic from having any sexual experiences. Rather it assures that whatever experiences he has will always be treated as "sin."[3]

To Enjoy the Body or To Master It?

Wait. I can hear you saying that in our culture men and boys enjoy their bodies. *They* are the ones who are so physical, who spend their time in sports, who compete. Exactly!—who compete. The absorption of the American male in bodily sports is not for enjoyment but for competition. There is enjoyment, but the absorption is in proving himself a man against other men. The body is for controlling, for subduing, for training to run faster or longer or better than others. The body is not for enjoying, for stroking, for responding. All this is for the genitals but not for the body as a whole. The body is for mastering and for mastering others.

The genitals are an interesting exception. Every man knows that his penis is the one part of his body which he fondles with the old tenderness and feeling which he had as a baby. Now as he masterbates or "has sex" he can "mother" himself with good feelings for his penis. Only here where he is unquestionably male does he allow himself to cherish his body.

Herb Goldberg, the author of *The Hazards of Being Male*, is clear how men relate to their bodies in general: "Most men operate as masochists and are constantly involved in proving something. They do little that feels good." Goldberg explains that men have body-destroying macho traits. They try to prove they can stand pain. They force themselves to be hyperactive and to resist or not admit fatigue. Men decline to seek a doctor's help. Men repress their emotions and are therefore vulnerable to alcohol, drugs and psychosomatic disorders. And their fear of their own bodily vulnerability keeps them from paying attention to their bodies.[4]

Rosemary Ruether notes that Freud as the founder of modern psychotherapy was not very helpful in changing our view of the body and sexuality. "He believed that culture creates a split between the tender, affectionate feelings and the sensual feelings, making it impossible to be fully sensual with those whom one respects, while making it necessary to degrade socially and morally those with whom one permits oneself free sensual activity. Freud held out little hope that this tendency could be overcome. For him sexual intercourse and the genitals were intrinsically disgusting and bestial to refined tastes, and so the tendency to split sensual from humane feelings was an almost inevitable casualty of culture. He notes curiously that this tendency appears primarily in men."[5]

Body/Self Dynamics in Maledom

"My long schooling in maledom has successfully separated my head from my body," writes Eugene Bianchi.[6] What does this separation do to the self? When men degrade their bodies, they in a strange way also degrade their own selfhood. Dorothy Dinnerstein speaks of "the animal center of self-respect: the brute sense of bodily prerogative, of having a right to one's bodily feelings." She sees that "a conviction that physical urges which one cannot help having are unjustified, undignified, presumptuous, undercuts the deepest, oldest basis for a sense of worth; it contaminates the original wellspring of subjective autonomy."[7] *When men degrade their bodies, they cut themselves off from this "original wellspring of subjective autonomy" and thus render their Real Self more fragile and insecure. This is what women sense and label as "the fragile male ego."*

Those body/self dynamics seem an extension of the male's early problem relating to his mother. All those good bodily feelings of being close, sucking the breast, being fed and warmed and loved all over—all those good body-feelings must be rejected as he seeks to pull away in order to establish that male ego which he will devote great energies to preserving and defending throughout his life.

Look at the male's situation through the categories of psychoanalyst Karen Horney once again (see chapter 5). Her analysis suggests that the male has left his infant Real Self—where his autonomy was related to and rooted in strong bodily feelings— back at his mother's breast in order to pursue an illusory Idealized Self laid upon him by our culture. When as a very small boy he started trying "not to cry" and "not to be a sissy," this involved his beginning to conform himself to an idealized model of what boys— and men—are supposed to be in our culture. It was not enough that he had been born with a penis (though one's masculinity might well be considered to have been given along with one's gender!). But when one's culture does not perceive it that way, then to *be* a man he must *become* a man—attain the strong, heroic, virile, almost Platonic ideal of masculinity which is presented by male socialization and the Masculine Mystique.

Because no actual human male can ever be this Idealized Male, each actual individual is never validated as having arrived, as having accomplished all that was required. A middle-aged husband in a Weber cartoon sees this when he tells his wife plaintively, "You expect too much from me. Basically, I'm just a dopey little kid from Mechanic Street, in Minneapolis, who happened to hit fifty."

Because of this lack of match between actual life history and the Idealized male Self, the man must try to prove himself daily, denying any pains or fears which as a human being with nerve-endings he may be feeling. Ironically, the more he approximates that Idealized male Self, the more he comes to have an identity separated from his body. He has thus drained his identity and selfhood of the power which would arise from real contact with his emotions and bodily feelings.

This self-alienation is then projected onto social relationships. Rosemary Ruether sees alienated and oppressive relations between people beginning "in self-alienation, experienced as an alienation between self and the body."

> The alienated oppressive relationship of man to woman is essentially a social projection of the self-alienation that translates certain initial

biological advantages into a power relationship. This power relationship is totalized in social structures and modes of cultural formation that eliminate woman's autonomous personhood to define her solely in terms of male needs.

In classical times this took the form of an identification of women with the lower half of self-alienated experience. Woman was stultifying matter opposing male spirituality. Woman was emotionality and sexuality opposing male spirituality. Woman was the power of the past, the immanent, the static, opposing male mobility and transcendence.

These images become self-fulfilling prophecies by socially incarnating and culturally enforcing them by excluding women from education and participation in public life and by immobilizing them in the home. By forbidding enlarging cultural experiences woman internalizes these images in herself. One shapes her to be what she symbolizes in the eye of self-alienated male perception.

Women become the victims of that very process by which the male seeks to triumph over the conflict represented by these dualities. Women were limited and repressed into that very sphere of immanence and materiality the male sought to escape, transcend and dominate.[8]

It is clear to me that men will never make it to centeredness and wholeness until they can claim as a part of themselves their own bodies and feelings. Men must come to grips with the symbols and psychic processes by which they have consciously or subconsciously pushed Body, Flesh, Carnality and Mortality away from themselves and onto Woman. We will never get over these particular hang-ups, Dorothy Dinnerstein suggests, until our sexual arrangements are changed and both men and women mutually and equally nurture children.

Bringing Body Reality to the Self

There has to be some strange irony that when I am ready to write this about our bodies and our selves, I am suddenly seized with a stomach virus and must collapse into bed for two days with severe abdominal discomfort. Am I being reminded that, as I present this new view of the body, I must include not only our enjoyment of the body-life but also the pain and suffering of body-life, and the limitations and aging of our bodies?

"Do not idealize the body," my aching abdomen reminds me. As I wrestle with the twin angels of inspiration and disease I realize that I don't want to idealize the body but to bring body-reality to the self. For too long we have deluded ourselves about our proper human identity. We have pretended our selfhood was only "clothed" in body, "dwelling" in body, unjustly "imprisoned" in body, while our immortal souls, our vast and beautiful selfhoods, could soar off to higher realms where baths were not necessary and where illness and pain, aging and dying, did not exist. What illusion! What pretension! What folly! All our loftiest dreams and most grand abstractions, as well as the most exquisite and intimate ecstacies of personhood—all are products of nerve endings, atoms and energy. "It is my belief," writes psychologist Herb Goldberg, "that an individual, in rhythm with his body and its needs, will thrive, and that 'the terrain is everything,' meaning the ability to listen to, respect, and respond to the demands of the body."[9] Such listening to our own bodies is a part of claiming our wholeness—accepting our flesh and our nerve endings instead of rejecting them, claiming our natural selves as a gift and not a curse.

A Broadly Sensuous and Erotic Encounter

What would it be like to appreciate our bodies, to live in the bodily dimensions of our personhoods as ones who cherish our creation as skin and muscle, hair and bone? Can we imagine ourselves into a space of understanding the goodness of our bodily creation as proclaimed by God in the Genesis account? Can we imagine ourselves "into" our bodies in a dimension that provides a whole new way of relating to the earth?

Let us begin by looking again at Penelope Washbourn's classic statement:

> I begin with my body. . . . my body is me. I can think of my body as a porous membrane, not separated from the world, as an organic body pulsing. . . opening and closing. . . taking in and giving out. It is like a flower as it turns to the sun, responds to light, growing, absorbing, expelling. . . . I am breathing gently and with such ease. . . until something happens to tense me, and my breath becomes shallow and labored. My skin is open, each of my cells in hair and skin is intimately connected to air, moisture, sun, dirt, hot and cold.[10]

Here is body as organism, not machine. Here is body open, not closed. Here is body intimately connected to all that surrounds it. The metaphor is openness and responsiveness rather than control or mastery.

I find in this passage by Penelope Washbourn a sensuousness of body awareness which suggests a way of relating ourselves beyond ourselves to our surroundings, our environment, our earth. The openness of nerve endings in skin and pores, in nose and ears and eyes, creates a dialogue with sun and wind, earth and water, in a highly interactive two-way process of non-verbal communication. The sun *feels* to me, the wind feels to me, the earth feels to me, the water feels to me. And as it feels, I respond, I enjoy, I take in and give out. I move and adapt to what I see and hear and feel and smell and sense. It is like a lover's dialogue; it needs no words in order to stroke and affirm, entice and arouse, assure and reassure.

As I write these words the sun and wind are caressing my entire body, while the plaintive cries of the gulls and the steady sound of waves reassure my ears of the continuities of the sea. The sand is rough and warm to my touch, and like ballet dancers the sea grasses wave and bend for my pleasure. The butterfly over the beach roses, the child digging on the beach, my son dipping and swaying as the sailboat planes in the magnificent breeze:—I am in non-verbal communication thorough my senses, through all of them. "With all people and all things, we shall be as relatives."

Kinship with brother earth and sister moon—St. Francis glimpsed it, but we have ignored that glimpse. Perhaps we could not love ourselves as bodies enough in that age to imagine this new organ of perception—the body. Perhaps it was historically necessary to wait for the contemporary hedonism of sexual liberation to shatter the old body-denying mind-sets before we could conceive the possibility of communicating with the earth through the sensuousness of our bodies.

Is it possible that this sensuality is the basic metaphor for the environmental ethic our culture has been missing? Is it possible that our fully sensuous body *is* the erotic connection to our world which we have been lacking? We know our living is part of the earth's living systems—that we are rooted in the earth and sensually in dialogue with it. Is it possible that intuitive wholistic awareness has as nerve endings our human skin?

I like the phrase I have heard attributed to Norman O. Brown, "the erotic sense of reality." Just suppose reality is at its heart truly erotic! Why else the symphonies of sight and sound and color and feeling which spell out creation well beyond what is necessary or useful? I am using the word "erotic" not in the genital-arousing sense but in the over-all and deeply sensual sense of generalized and heightened responsiveness and sensitivity. The poem "For Warmth," by Elise Maclay, suggests the body-to-body eroticism in the varied tactile appreciations of an elderly person's earthy experiences of temperature. To my mind, it is deeply sensuous and erotic.

Thanks, God, for warmth.
For the sun coming up like hope,
Like joy in the morning,
Laying a gentle hand on my hair,
Melting the sharpness of the world.
Thanks, God, for warmth.
For warm clothes, warm rooms,
A warm bed.
For warm-bodied animals. Cats. Dogs.
Warm water to wash in,
Tea, soup, warm bread,
A fire on the hearth,
Warm friendships,
Kindness from a stranger.
Thanks, God, for warmth.
It feels like Your smile.[11]

If reality is erotic, perhaps we can only glimpse its heart with our own erotic nature. Perhaps our body is the only communicator we have for this sort of non-verbal love play with the body of the earth. Perhaps cherishing the earth means participating in a broadly sensuous encounter between the body of the earth and our own bodies. And perhaps as process theology suggests, the cosmos is the body of God.

Snow

The tall lithe figure of the young skier came whipping over the crest. His legs were together, his skis parallel, his knees constantly flexing as he jumped from mogul to mogul, rhythmically turning again and again as he sped down the slope. It was a magnificent skiing day—several inches of fresh white powder, bright sunlight and blue skies after the snow the previous night. But the most startling thing was the sound. The skier was singing, exulting and exuberant, as he skied. The coordination of his body, its instant responses to the changes in the terrain beneath his skis, made him feel in dialogue with the earth as it changed its shape beneath him. And the brightness of the day, the freshness of the snow, the perfectness of the ski conditions, the beauty of the mountains—all evoked exuberant singing as he went. It was a time of dialogue and he knew it. It was a time of rejoicing and he knew it. It was an unforgettable moment. He was my son and he told me when he returned: "It was just an excellent day for skiing, Mom, and I sang all the way down."

Wind and Rain

One of my husband's great joys is to go out in our small sailboat when the wind is blowing whitecaps onto the crests of waves. The boat is slender and fast, its sails converting the wind of successive gusts into swift motion. The boat and sails bend under the wind, the boat tilts even as he secures his toes under a hiking strap and leans far, far out to windward until his hair and back are skimming inches above the waves and his stomach muscles are aching. They are in the wind's embrace, the boat and he, and they are active lovers. His every pore is wet, his eyeglasses starred with salt and spray.

But there is no need to see. He can feel the surge of the hull against the waves, feel the lift of the hull as it heels up beneath him even as he feels an increased intensity of wind tingling his flesh all over. When the wind heightens and the boat heels like this, he can take the boat and the sails slightly closer to his lover wind and crest the waves just slightly differently. Pressures of the wind upon the hull and tiller and waves and sails ease at his changed response—and they fly on. But then the gust's intensity abates, and lover-like he moves to return to the full embrace. He and the boat "bear off" enough to keep the sails solid, the movement of the boat in the waves and wind firm, and the dialogue of responsiveness alive.[12]

"In some strange sense," we read in *The Tao of Physics*, "the universe is a participatory universe."[13] What an incredible idea! The universe relates back to us even as we respond to it. But it all happens without words, in "body-language" if you will. And if you don't speak body-language, if you understand only the code of spoken language and the abstractions of print and the written word, how will you ever play this love-game with the world?

*   *   *

Your name is called in the middle of the night. You wake, unexpectedly, answering automatically to that strange call whispered in childhood, sung in adolescence, echoed in adulthood. You rise to the window with the same excitement, so strangely understood yet unspoken, that you felt on these early morning childhood journeys bound for places still nameless, still memoryless.

Rain, soft and sibilant, calls you in the middle of the night. It calls you, passenger of the night, to witness the world awash with rain. You watch a world made new, a work declaring itself sovereign.

You pause there at the window which frames the garden in darkness. Softened by the rain, the garden breathes as gently, as rhythmically as those who still are fast asleep. Like a nocturnal fruit cracked open and cleansed by the rain, the earth emits an extravagance of smells, living in memory, hidden by day and scorned by season. In the rain, rock and root yield a ransom of smells from the bankrupt garden: fresh cucumber, washed woodbine, perfumed muskrose, tart orange.

In the darkness, smells thicken into colors. A profusion of orange blossoms become a moving, muted orange which swells in the air; the wild mint, so indiscriminate in its homesteading, spins and stings with greenness; and the pears, heavy with their own scent, burn golden in the darkness of night.

All week you stood at this same window and conjured up water images in a rainless sky. The sun had flickered in that sky like a young salmon whose silver scales shine and darken, quicken and quiver with the undulation of its movements. Then darkness had set in. The sky you thought looked like the gray bottom of a boat moored close above the earth. Water images in a rainless sky. What use were they when the sky felt scalded, the air parched, the earth cracked? That night when you went to bed, your hands strangely smelt of salt.

And now, hours later, rain has united sky and earth, stitching them together with fine filaments of sound. In the darkness, rain has become both sound and silence. Moment and memory, waking and sleeping self are united by this liquid language. Syllables of rain publish themselves in the garden.

You lift your face skywards. The air faintly smells of melon. You smile; your face as grateful as a prayer. You give silent thanks for the rain, this epiphany, this euphony.[14]

Life as Love-Game and Erotic Embrace

The Hebrews had a sense of this knowing without words, this love-game of life in which world and self and loved companion become present, revealed, known, and fondly savored. In Hebrew, a single word, *yada*, meant both "to make sexual love" and "to know." This Old Testament usage would puzzle recent generations more used to casual sex. Rosemary Ruether has said of recent trends, "One makes love with genitals, not selves."[15]

Recently I have come to suspect that the splitting of sex and love for the sake of ennobling "love" and "respect for women" is really a cultural lie that covers up what it is we really fear most. I suspect that what males (who have been the cultural shapers of these attitudes) fear most is not sexual experience but rather ego-vulnerability through communication of the inner self.... Masculinist society segregates itself from women so profoundly that even in the sexual act it is difficult to express real interpersonalism. The male operates within a self-enclosed world that reduces the woman sexually to a vehicle for himself, rather than being a fellow person. Sex depersonalized allows the male to avoid the challenge of using his total self, uniting energies with personal identities, to present and communicate one to another.

*   *   *

Self-surrender is treated by the male as a threat to control of "his world," rather than a potential release into a larger world than the monistic self. This seems to me to be the dynamics that cause men to hold back from real self-disclosure in sexual experience. The self is split from the body, and the body then can be manipulated as an external instrument of domination in a way that does not threaten to dissolve the defenses of the ego....To open oneself to deep vulnerability and communication is profoundly terrifying, especially when it is unified with sexual experience as a total body-potential that transforms communion into ecstasy.[16]

It is this deep self-disclosure and communication which the Old Testament calls "sexual knowing." This may indeed be the sort of knowing by which the body of a person resonates with the body of the earth, by which communion becomes ecstasy, and by which both knower and known reveal themselves and the depths of their connectedness.

Note that in this knowing and intercourse, it is not intercourse as patriarchal male culture has structured it, in which there is an active one and a passive one, a penetrator and a penetrated. Nor is such intercourse focused, as males have tended to, solely upon the genitals. Rather, this intercourse is diffused and evokes the sensuality of both bodies, and is incredibly mutual, dynamically interactive, and responsive. Perhaps in order to know the reality of our earthy universe we must know sexuality in this way—where there is no separation between the active one and the passive one, the penetrator and the penetrated, but where lovers in each others' embrace are resonant with one another in a sensuous and deeply erotic union which is mutually dynamic and responsive.

And finally perhaps in the liberating "knowing" of the earth, we may come to know ourselves, male and female, in a finally liberated way. Perhaps when we honor our bodies and the body of the earth, we shall honor women and all life in a new way.

11.

A Proper Sense of Death

There is something in us that doesn't ever want to let go to face even as inevitable a fact as a new season. Some people cling and cling like the oak leaves that hold on till next spring and the new ones push them off.

Last night flocks of wild geese flew over our house. In my half sleep I heard them honking. Unerringly they follow the rhythm of the seasons—their instinct telling them when to leave for southern climates. Some may not make the trip back and yet all go in good grace. Their great wide V stretches over the heavens, momentarily putting out the stars as they pass. When we human beings let go and embrace the new, when we flow with the seasons, and merge with the same basic rhythm that tells the geese when to go, we hear things beyond sound, and feel things beyond touch, and a kind of serenity settles over our spirits.[1]

A Proper Sense of Death

To do this—to claim the gift of life—we must also claim a new understanding of death. In the Genesis myth all the goodness of life was put within the Garden and then it was all cursed with pain, suffering and death in the Fall. Of course the myth gave woman a starring role in the Fall, as suddenly man's derivative and dependent helpmate Eve became a major character who in sinning exhibited both initiative and masculine aggressiveness while ending the whole Utopian scene.

Besides being used for centuries against women, the story of the Fall has served to distort our understanding of both death and human life. Rather than dying being as integral to human life as being born, Death became a Curse "which might not have been," a punishment for sin, a sort of lethal and arbitrary celestial "ZAP." Death became the Enemy, something apart from our true nature, something we could not claim as a part of our human pilgrimage. Over the centuries it has been easier for us to view ourselves (as

Ernest Becker does) as "gods with anuses," because we have never "owned" or "claimed" dying as a part of our humanity.

We are today engaged in many quarters in a reappraisal of death. I want to present now three examples of such reappraisals, the first by Lewis Thomas, president of Memorial Sloan-Kettering Cancer Center in New York City:

> [Death] is a natural marvel. All of the life of the earth dies, all of the time, in the same volume as the new life that dazzles us each morning, each spring. All we see of this is the odd stump, the fly struggling on the porch floor of the summer house in October, the fragment on the highway. I have lived all my life with an embarrassment of squirrels in my backyard, they are all over the place, all year long, and I have never seen, anywhere, a dead squirrel.

> I suppose it is just as well. If the earth were otherwise, and all the dying were done in the open, with the dead there to be looked at, we would never have it out of our minds. We can forget about it much of the time, or think of it as an accident to be avoided, somehow. But it does make the process of dying seem more exceptional than it really is, and harder to engage in at the times when we must ourselves engage.

> *   *   *

> There are 3 billion of us on the earth, and all 3 billion must be dead, on a schedule, within this lifetime.

> *   *   *

> We will have to give up the notion that death is catastrophe, or detestable, or avoidable, or even strange. We will need to learn more about the cycling of life in the rest of the system, and about our connection to the process. Everything that comes alive seems to be in trade for something that dies, cell for cell. There might be some comfort in the recognition of synchrony, in the information that we all go down together, in the best of company.

> *   *   *

> We may be about to rediscover that dying is not such a bad thing to do after all. Sir William Osler took this view: he disapproved of people who spoke of the agony of death, maintaining that there was no such thing.

> *   *   *

> [David Livingston, based upon his own experience of near-death while in Africa] was so amazed by the extraordinary sense of peace, calm, and total painlessness associated with being killed that he contructed a theory that all creatures are provided with a protective physiologic mechanism, switched on at the verge of death, carrying them through in a haze of tranquility. I have seen agony in death only once, in a patient with rabies.... It was as though, in the special neuropathology of rabies, the switch had been prevented from turning.

*   *   *

I find myself surprised by the thought that dying is an all-right thing to do, but perhaps it should not surprise. It is, after all, the most ancient and fundamental of biologic functions, with its mechanisms worked out with the same attention to detail, the same provision for the advantage of the organism, the same abundance of genetic information for guidance through the stages, that we have long since become accustomed to finding in all the crucial acts of living.[2]

Another who has been involved in a contemporary reappraisal of death and has helped a great many with their own grief and dying is Elisabeth Kuebler-Ross. Writing in her book *Death: The Final Stage of Growth,* she says:

Experiencing, rather than being shielded from, death, I have been able to understand it as an expected and integral part of life.

*   *   *

I am convinced that these experiences with the reality of death have enriched my life more than any other experiences I have had. Facing death means facing the ultimate question of the meaning of life. If we really want to live we must have the courage to recognize that life is ultimately very short, and that everything we do counts.[3]

Fontaine Belford has written about the place of death in literature, and about the differing place which death holds in comedy and tragedy:

The most fundamental definition of comedy and tragedy is that a comedy is a play ending in marriage, a tragedy a play ending in death. The feminine with its emphasis on the species, the race, focused on the life which biologically did not end, the cosmic chain of birth and death and birth. It was comic. The masculine with its focus on the individual and his own private and personal life and destiny, faces the death which will end it. Each of our separate plays will end in death, but the great play will go on. Tragedy and comedy![4]

Perhaps it has been this inability to accept death into a cosmic comic view of life which has enticed men into rejecting the limitations of humanity and into struggling instead "to be as gods." But the Tower of Babel which civilized man has erected consists not in the height of his walls and towers but in the power of his machines to articulate his will. Charles Ferguson has described this development in man's spirit:

It was natural if not inevitable that man's accomplishments should induce in him. . .a voluptuous self-esteem. From an idealization of the machine, he began to move toward an idolization of himself. His power appeared to be infinite. The think machine was early seen to be abler than man in some particulars and rapidly capable of becoming superior. Yet man had created it. Was he not moving rapidly along a path toward infallibility when he might be no longer merely a creator but equal to the Creator?[5]

At another point Ferguson describes the jet airliner as a daily miracle-reminder to man of his abilities:

After a few breathless moments on the runway, the passenger seems to ascend personally. Then he is where he has longed to be for ages— in the sky and above the earth. Right at hand he may have pie in the sky or towering ice cream sodas stacked endlessly. Or he may see the shadow of the plane on the clouds below, caught in a moving halo that keeps pace with the movement of man, to assure him of his glory. Man on top. It is his supreme achievement. So far. A little higher than the angels. The Psalms improved. Man as god, just as he foresaw he would be. Nature, man's old enemy, reduced to a woolly euphemism called turbulence.[6]

Western experience has been haunted through the centuries by the Genesis account which has labeled us fallen, in the bondage of Death, and separated from the original gift of life. The Fall has been thought of as downward—from grace to some lower and more sinful (and mortal) state. But perhaps this must be re-thought. It may have been a fall *up* into anthropocentric pretention and illusion—up into thinking man could get beyond death, beyond flesh, beyond nature, and really be "on top." And in attempting to be as gods, we have not properly valued being human.

*   *   *

In *A Second Birthday* the lay theologian William Stringfellow writes about how his own long struggle with pain, sickness and nearness to death brought him to a newly dawning sense of life, what he calls his "second birthday." Of this he says:

Vocation has to do with recognizing life as a gift and honoring the gift in living.

*   *   *

In the Gospel, vocation means being a human being, now, and being neither more, nor less than a human being, now.

*   *   *

Worship is the celebration of life in its totality.

He writes of the place of self-love in what others, expressing their gratitude for his recovery from death, call a miracle:

> Self-love is decisive. I do not mean, by that, a strenuous will to live. I refer to a reality which is, indeed, rather the opposite: a love of self which, esteeming life itself as a gift, expects or demands no more than the life which is given, and which welcomes and embraces and affirms that much unconditionally. I mean self-love which emulates, and, in the end, participates in, the love of God for life.[7]

Life Itself Is the Gift

In a strange way, when we fail to accept death, we miss the gift of life. In our striving to "be god," we miss what it is to be human.

*   *   *

> Each day is a beginning.
> Each day I am new.

*   *   *

> To pull the blinds of habit from the eyes,
> to see the world without names for the first bright time,
> to wander through its mystery, to wonder
> at every age and stage, at one with it—
> to be alive![8]

Jean Hersey speaks of the priceless gift of "living in the moment" which she receives from the visit of her grandson.

> I always learn so much from my young visitor that many a new door opens. Perhaps the most valuable thing I learn relates to the special joy that lies in each moment. Every day for us becomes a succession of nows. Spring is eons away; last fall doesn't exist. The past may be wonderful to ruminate on and draw strength from, the future exciting, thrilling to anticipate, to plan for; but the present, the "now," is the only time we are really alive. This very moment is actually all we ever have. Of this Jesse forcefully reminds me. Even "next week" produces a vague look in his eyes, and when I talk about last week, I have lost him. He is studying a small black cricket that is crawling over the rug, and last week—what is that?[9]

Everything Created Is Vulnerable

In a strange way, only when we face the vulnerability of created life and can accept that vulnerability, can we claim the real gift of life in the "now." It is when we are still fighting off death that we launch vast campaigns of "achieving," which focus on the future and hurry us past a real tasting or feeling of what we are experiencing in this moment.

Huston Smith speaks of this thrust of achieving—"this dream of onward and upward," he calls it—which has been so prominent in our Western civilization:

> If within this vast universe a thread of life were to angle always upward, leaving a trail that looked from a distance like the jet stream of an ascending plane, such a never-circling life force would be a freak. For everywhere else—name one exception—nature favors the curves that space itself conforms to; the yin-yang rhythms of turning gyres and waves that crest and fall.
>
> O my people! can you not see how it is hope, not fact, that powers this dream of onward and upward toward the dawning light? *If human life is truly natural*—and this, surely, the evolutionists would want us to believe—*it is seasonal*. Fall and winter are its lot as assuredly as summer and spring. Half the art of living is a talent for dying.[10] (Emphasis added.)

In *Plant Dreaming Deep* May Sarton writes of the gardener's sense of seasonal change:

> For the joys a garden brings are already going as they come. They are poignant. When the first apple falls with that tremendous thud, one of the big seasonal changes startles the heart. The swanlike peony suddenly lets all its petals fall in a snowy pile, and it is time to say good-by until another June. But by then the delphinium is on the way and the lilies...[for] the flowers ring their changes through a long cycle, a cycle that will be renewed.
>
> That is what the gardner often forgets. To the flowers we never have to say good-by forever. *We* grow older every year, but not the garden; it is reborn every spring.[11] (Emphasis added.)

Accepting creation is accepting that seasonal quality to life, accepting the fall and winter of life just as we enjoy the spring. It is accepting the whole arc of a life span, the curve down into fragility as well as the curve up into vigor. It is accepting the blessing in mortal flesh, which is a temporary blessing. In order to get the blessing, we must take into ourselves the temporary quality of it, and claim that also as our own.

A doctor friend of Elisabeth Kuebler-Ross writes in *Death: The Final Stage of Growth* about his own acceptance of that temporary quality in the period after his surgeon told him, "It was a malignant tumor." He has just been speaking of being impressed by "the grace of that young Irish American surgeon and saint who started the medical aid program to Southeast Asia, as he faced his own terminal malignancy."

> Through Tom Dooley, two real options became vividly real. The answer to "How much time do I have?" became "There are 'x' days left and, however long 'x' is, there are only two possibilities, to live them in despair or to really live them to the hilt, making them count, as Dooley did." The choice was clear and a great weight was lifted from my shoulders. It would be impossible to exaggerate the significance of that moment. It led to the next realization, that really we're all in the same boat, with 'x' days to live. Even if cured of the cancer, I'm a day closer to dying today than yesterday. We all are. For all of us then, it isn't the quantity of life but the quality that counts. It took a malignancy to put life into perspective....[12]

The Rhythm of Life

Why is it so hard for us to accept the rhythms of mortal life? Fritjof Capra in *The Tao of Physics* writes: "Modern physics has shown that the rhythm of creation and destruction is not only manifest in the turn of the seasons and in the birth and death of all living creatures, but is also the very essence of inorganic matter. According to quantum field theory, all interactions between the constituents of matter take place through the emission and absorption of virtual particles. More than that, the dance of creation and destruction is the basis of the very existence of matter, since all material particles 'self-interact' by emitting and reabsorbing virtual particles. *Modern physics has thus revealed that every subatomic particle not only performs an energy dance, but also is an energy dance; a pulsating process of creation and destruction.*"[13] (Emphasis added.)

Life is a rhythm of creation and destruction. Human life is seasonal, as Huston Smith puts it. Thus there must be not only "a time to be born" but also "a time to die"; a time to be young, and a time to age. If we understand what it is to be human (i.e., seasonal), we can taste and savor each season in its own time as Mrs. Miniver does in Jan Struther's novel:

It was lovely, thought Mrs. Miniver, nodding goodbye to the flower-woman and carrying her big sheaf of chrysanthemums down the street with a kind of ceremonious joy, as though it were a cornucopia; it was lovely, this settling down again, this tidying away of the summer into its box, this taking up of the thread of one's life where the holidays (irrelevant interlude) had made one drop it. Not that she didn't enjoy the holidays: but she always felt—and it was, perhaps, the measure of her peculiar happiness—a little relieved when they were over. Her normal life pleased her so well that she was half afraid to step out of its frame in case one day she should find herself unable to get back. The spell might break, the atmosphere be impossible to recapture.

But this time, at any rate, she was safe. There was the house, as neat and friendly as ever.... And there was the square itself, with the leaves still as thick on the trees as they had been when she left in August; but in August they had hung heavily, a uniform dull green, whereas now, crisped and brindled by the first few nights of frost, they had taken on a new, various beauty. Stepping lightly and quickly down the square, Mrs. Miniver suddenly understood why she was enjoying the forties so much better than she had enjoyed the thirties: it was the difference between August and October, between the heaviness of late summer and the sparkle of early autumn, between the ending of an old phase and the beginning of a fresh one.

*   *   *

Upstairs in the drawing-room there was a small bright fire of logs, yet the sunshine that flooded in through the open windows had real warmth in it. It was perfect: she felt suspended between summer and winter, savoring the best of them both. She unwrapped the chrysanthemums and arranged them in a square glass jar, between herself and the light, so that the sun shone through them. They were the big mop-headed kind, burgundy-colored, with curled petals; their beauty was noble, architectural; and as for their scent, she thought as she buried her nose in the nearest of them, it was a pure distillation of her mood, a quintessence of all that she found gay and intoxicating and astringent about the weather, the circumstances, her own age and the season of the year. Oh yes, October certainly suited her best.[14]

"Green Winter"

But what of aging? Can we accept that weakening of the muscle fiber, that decline in vigor, that loneliness of those who remain for those who have gone? What indeed can one savor in a season that is peopled largely by the absences of those who once were, a season that is "the glass mostly empty"?

Preserve me from the occupational therapist, God,
She means well, but I'm too busy to make baskets.
I want to relive a day in July
When Sam and I went berrying.
I was eighteen,
My hair was long and thick
And I braided it and wound it round my head
So it wouldn't get caught on the briars,
But when we sat down in the shade to rest
I unpinned it and it came tumbling down,
and Sam proposed.
I suppose it wasn't fair
To use my hair to make him fall in love with me,
But it turned out to be a good marriage,
And years later when our daughter said
She thought she'd cut her hair,
I said, "Oh don't. There's something
Mystical about long hair. If after a year
You still want to cut it, do, but think it
Over." A year later,
She said, "Oh Mom, I'm so glad you told me not to
    cut my hair,
Jeff loves it so."
Oh, here she comes, the therapist, with scissors and paste.
Would I like to try decoupage?
"No," I say, "I haven't got time."
"Nonsense," she says, "you're going to live a long,
    long time."
That's not what I mean,
I mean that all my life I've been doing things
For people, with people, I have to catch up
On my thinking and feeling.
About Sam's death, for one thing.
At the time there were so many things to do,
So many people around,
I had to keep assuring everyone I'd be all right,
I had to eat and make sure they noticed,
So they wouldn't keep coming to see me when
They had other things to do.
I had to comfort the children
And Sam's old friends who got scared
(If Sam could die, they could die, too).
I had to give his clothes away and pay the bills,
I didn't have time to think about how brave he was,
How sweet. One day,
Close to the end, I asked if there was anything I could do,
He said, "Yes, unpin your hair."
I said, "Oh, Sam, it's so thin now and gray."
"Please," he said, "unpin it anyway."

I did and he reached out his hand—
The skin transparent, I could see the blue veins—
And stroked my hair.
If I close my eyes, I can feel it. Sam.
"Please open your eyes," the therapist says,
"You don't want to sleep the day away."
As I say, she means well,
She wants to know what I used to do,
Knit? Crochet?
Yes, I did all those things,
And cooked and cleaned
And raised five children,
And had things happen to me.
Beautiful things, terrible things,
I need to think about them,
At the time there wasn't time,
I need to sort them out,
Arrange them on the shelves of my mind.
The therapist is showing me glittery beads,
She asks if I might like to make jewelry.
Her eyes are as bright as the beads,
She's a dear child and she means well,
So I tell her I might
Some other day.[15]

As I read those words I am overcome with tenderness for my own Sam, also grayer and more vulnerable than when we too first let down our hair to each other, but so much more precious to me because I now understand the human limitedness of our time together. I want to rush in to where he is sleeping and waken him to celebrate the present moment which is slipping by with the liquid speed of the Mozart piano nocturne I have playing on the phonograph. But we will waken together to greet the sea and the morning, and that will be time.

*   *   *

"Grandfather, does the water go on a long way?" "Yes, boy, further than you or I can imagine." "Is the water old then?" "Neither old nor young. It just goes on."

"Will I be as old as you are? Will I be as old as that frog? What is it like to be old?" "It is all just floating on the water, on and on."

"Grandfather, what is this?"

"It is called milkweed, boy. Let it fly."

"Look, it goes up and up. Is it alive?" "Yes, in its way. Can you still see it?"

"It's higher than the birds. I've lost it now. I wish I could fly."

"You will, boy, in your way."

"Grandfather, tell me about flying. Tell me about water. Tell me about everything. Tell me what it is, to be alive."[16]

The Supreme Quality of Being Transitory

I don't mean by all this that we should enjoy dying. I don't think we enjoy being born. But both are natural, and a proper part of human life. Death is a fitting and proper destiny for the human—a part of the arc and span of being mortal flesh.

*   *   *

Swathed in coats and scarves, they went out and sat in a row on the little flagged terrace. The evening might have been ordered with the fireworks; it was cold, still, and starry, with a commendable absence of moon. And when the first rocket went up Mrs. Miniver felt the customary pricking in her throat and knew that once again the enchantment was going to work. Some things—conjurers, ventriloquists, pantomimes—she enjoyed vicariously, by watching the children's enjoyment; but fireworks had for her a direct and magical appeal. Their attraction was more complex than that of any other form of art. They had pattern and sequence, color and sound, brilliance and mobility; they had suspense, surprise, and a faint hint of danger; above all, they had the supreme quality of transcience, which puts the keenest edge on beauty and makes it touch some spring in the heart which more enduring excellences cannot reach.[17]

12.

Woman as Bearer of a
Different Consciousness

I know I am most content when my days are filled with a constant
awareness of the sun rising and setting, of leaves unfolding in spring,
flourishing in summer and dropping in the fall. I find my spirit
thrives when close to the ebb and flow of Nature's tides.[1]

Experiencing the Ebb and Flow

"It has long been an aspiration of men," Robert Jay Lifton and
Eric Olson write in *Living and Dying*, "to experience the ebb and
flow of human existence as rhythmically as the passages and
changes in the rest of nature."[2] This may be an aspiration of men—
but clearly it has been difficult for men to accomplish. Why?

*When I contrast "male" and "female," I do not mean to make the
contrast between stereotypic "masculine" and "feminine" traits.*

I do not observe that all men are active (and all women passive), or all
men intellectual (and all women emotional), or all men achievers
(while all women are nurturers). Thousands of lives, both male and
female, contradict those generalizations. It is clear that both men and
women have what I think are better seen as *human* capabilities to
think and feel, to achieve and nurture, to love and hate and aspire
and fear, and so on. Of course these capabilities are present in
different degrees (and developed to different degrees) in different
individuals. Thus the similarities in our human capabilities far
outweigh our differences as males and females.

Having gone this far in turning aside from stereotypic differences
between "masculine" and "feminine," I want also to be clear that *I do
not in any way mean to imply that male and female are absolutely the
same,* for it is obvious that they are not. *What the actual (non-
stereotypic) differences between males and females may be, however,
is something we as a culture are only beginning to clarify and
research.*

Because (as Lewis Perelman has observed in quite another connection) "Consciousness is experience;...one's consciousness *is* what one 'experiences.'"[3]

Let us begin by looking at what bodily experiences the man does and does not have. Puberty brings to him strength and vigor and sexual appetite and performance. It does not however bring to a normally healthy male any bodily experiences of weakness, limit, or intrinsic connection to natural processes. In short, the male bodily experience is quite lacking in experiences which would help him forge an adequate world view or relationship to nature or concept of limits.

Contrast that with the bodily experience of the woman (an experience and "consciousness" which has never been allowed by patriarchal society to be expressed as a world view). For more than forty years the cycles of menstruation move every month through her emotional and physical system, bringing with them her own particular version of weakness, fatigue, pre-menstrual tension, and cramps. No matter how much she might like to view herself as an individual unit with a world view that stops at her own skin, her bodily selfhood is invaded every month by lunar cycles which come with monotonous regularity, whether she wishes children or not, so that she experiences the surging tides of human reproduction which flow in potential through her body. I myself have menstruated more than 480 times so far for the privilege of having two children, a bit of natural overkill that reminds me of the sorts of firepower used in the Vietnam War!

It is clear that males and females *experience a life journey from within bodies which differ physically*. Men have long been clear how women's experience was shaped and limited by having a vagina and uterus. We are only beginning to perceive how men's experience is shaped and limited by having a penis and testicles. The male life-experience has saturated the intellectual and technological spaces of our culture and has been the assumed norm and referent. But it is the feminists in academia, for example, who have noted the omnipresence of phrases about "the thrust of his argument" or about someone's "penetrating statement." One also notes with humor that when a computer is working it is "up" and when it is unable to compute it is "down." Yet the pervasiveness of this male physical "viewing point" not only in our language but in our ways of thinking and in our artifacts has been scarcely noted, let alone its limitations realistically assessed. Perhaps the reason is that males by themselves have been unable to do this.

> *Occupying a male (or female) body means that male (or female)*
> *hormones predominate in that body's hormonal "climate."* The
> effects of these differences in our bodies is only beginning to be
> understood. For example, it has been ascertained that males as a
> group have a superior grasp of spatial relationships. Recent research
> has suggested that this is a consequence of the presence of the male
> hormone testosterone. On the other hand, the synchrony in monthly
> menstrual cycles among women living or working together has
> recently been determined to be a function of females' capacity to
> perceive and attune involuntarily to certain body odors of those
> around them.

So the first point about female bodily experience of menstruation
is that it provides an inescapable limit upon her physical existence,
to which she must learn to adapt and to live within. It would be
difficult for such a woman to dream up a sense of herself as
unlimited or as all-conquering mind or as a Promethean self. Such
dreams of glory come crashing down the next time her body
experiences the monthly limit. There is no such experience for man
unless he is sick or crippled—which most of our male decision-
makers and thinkers are not.

Menstruation also provides woman with an inescapable sense of
connection to the natural world, a sense which is further heightened
by the experiences (if she becomes a mother) of pregnancy and
childbirth. This inevitable involvement of the woman with the
processes of nature that flow through her body is both conscious
and unconscious. There are some deep levels of connection. The
pull of the moon upon the tides is common knowledge. There is
beginning to be evidence that people bleed more at the full of the
moon, so that some surgeons are now refusing to do major
operations at that time. There is some evidence that mental illnesss
(which, you will recall, used to be called "lunacy") peaks at the full
of the moon. But what has not been investigated, I am informed, is
the relation of women's menstrual cycles to lunar cycles. I know that
I am perfectly sychronized with lunar cycles, and when I get "off" I
experience ovulation pains, and only then! There is also increasing
evidence about women who live together (college dorms, mothers
and daughters): even though they begin on different menstrual
cycles, their cycles over a period of time come to coincide. Some
deep connections to the natural world do seem to flow through the
bodily life of the woman, and she has some deep or subliminal

senses of these connections which have never been expressed as a comprehensive world view.

What Our Bodies Teach

I see nothing like this in the life of the man. Rather, the male bodily experience is of a *lack* of such connectedness—which is exactly what the masculine consciousness expresses. And, I would ask, could it be otherwise? Can the world view cast up by males express a connection with nature which nothing in their bodily experience causes them to know and feel in their bones and nerves and bowels?

Or take the sense of caring about future generations. It does not seem to me accidental that the dominant paradigm today does not concern itself about the life of future generations. What is there in the bodily experience of the male which might cause him to feel involved in future generations? The male's one function of providing the semen is overwhelmed by the exploding sensation of orgasm, a sexual satisfaction he seeks innumerable times, in many contexts, and often with little reference to human reproduction. And that is his entire *bodily* experience of producing the next generation!

Contrast that with the woman's dawning awareness of the new life growing *within* her, carried by her body, nourished by her blood, kicking and turning, gestating with the slow ripening of natural cycles which seem interminable near the end. Finally that new life within her is ejected laboriously and with herculean movements of her uterus and birth canal to begin its first life apart from her body. Now, ask *that* woman to cast up a world view that ignores the life of the next generation!

Or take women's intuitive understanding of short-term pleasure (making love) and long-term cost (producing and then rearing a child). Women during puberty come to awareness of the long-term parameters of their sexual encounters, and if they do not immediately understand, they pay the price for their lack of comprehension. There is no comparable biological occasion for helping men overcome their penchant for taking short-term profit and exporting the long-term costs to others—women, other social groups, or the environment. And women's consciousness, which is so beautifully but painfully programmed by her childbearing potential to understand the long-term consequences of short-term actions, has not been allowed into the board rooms and our society's centers of policy-making.

The different socialization of males and females constitutes a third major cause of observed male/female differences. Men have been taught to be strong, never cry, aspire to success, "prove their masculinity," and so on. Women, on the other hand, are allowed to feel hurt, to cry, to feel vulnerable. Women are encouraged to succeed vicariously and feel successful when they help and nurture a child or husband or boss—someone *else*—who succeeds. And women are socialized to feel successful themselves when they are loved. Males, on the other hand, are *not* socialized to feel successful when they are loved. Differing male/female socialization experiences are a major part of why many adult men experience difficulty expressing feelings of fear or inadequacy or dependence. Adult women characteristically have their difficulty when trying to define themselves as autonomous, aspiring and inner-directed adults.

Cultural patterns of male/female socialization both produce and reinforce "masculine/feminine" stereotypes. So cultural stereotypes about what constitute masculine or feminine traits not only color the experience of us all, but they also cloud our seeing precisely which of the observed male-female differences are biologically-grounded and which are, instead, culturally induced.

In summary: to contrast male and female is to contrast different (1) *bodily physical experiences,* different (2) *hormonal climates in those physical bodies,* and different (3) *experiences of sex-linked socialization.* The contrasting of males and females has been done in the past by cultures dominated by males. Furthermore, the principal assessments have never been done in order to perceive the limitations of males' own physical experience—the life-realities which a penis-bound bodily experience does not permit one to perceive or grasp. If these assessments were to have purely personal consequences, we could all afford our blind-spots and foibles. But what we are speaking of are the ways in which men's (and male-dominated cultures') particular window upon reality is incomplete and insufficient—and currently constitutes a danger to human survival. If no other human viewing point were available, then "that would be that." But happily for our species, such need not be the case.

A Biologically Conditioned Consciousness

I am asserting that there is a definite limit to the perception of men. It is a limit imposed upon their consciousness by the lack of certain bodily experiences which are present in the life of a woman.

No matter how androgynous men may become, it is therefore not possible for men alone to lead us into a society with a fully developed sense of its limited but harmonious place in nature. It is not possible for men alone to do this because the male's is simply a much diminished experience of body, of natural processes, and of future generations. I do not by this mean to downgrade men but only to point out their limitation. I also do not want to romanticize the bodily experiences of women. For me and for many women these have not been altogether pleasant experiences. But, pleasant or unpleasant, these have been powerful learning experiences. And they are experiences which do have a powerful molding effect upon women's consciousness and view of the world—in ways I do not see even approximated in the life of males.

*   *   *

Audrey Drummond writes about the shaping of a woman's consciousness by her woman's bodily experiences:

Think of the profound times of the female body. . . menstruation. . . childbearing. . . menopause. The necessities of her body are never trivial. They are deep with meaning.

On the day of her first menstruation she is ready for childbearing. There is no chronological time. There is no rabbi or priest to welcome her with ritual. It is her body that decides when it is her time.

Then, when—and if—she decides to let another enter her body sexually, she must accept the physical act as well as the psychological concept of an outside force within her own body.

If she should decide to become pregnant, she must ready herself for another intrusion. If she is ready, she opens herself to the sperm, letting it flow in and absorbing it, but always holding on to her inner being.

As the zygote grows, the intrusion into her body can be overwhelming as she feels a body within her own body. Two hearts are beating in one body!

Yet the woman must stay centered as her body yields to another's demands. It is the first thought of the infinite, body within body.

In its time, when the babe feels it can no longer be sustained by the mother's body, there is a separation. The babe moves out into its own space and time.

The woman and the child join then with all living beings in an infinite chain—past, present and future. Human life is seen in sequence, one after another, each life having its place in time. Remember this as you think of this human chain of ancestors. We see this chain as the passing of time because our selective bodies have taken the cosmic moving whole and stilled it into fragments.

But there is still one more stage for woman and that is her menopause, the time when her body no longer prepares itself for childbirth.

At that time woman acknowledges the passing of time and sees herself as an ancestor. Death becomes acceptable as part of the time chain. For she sees the chain of ancestors reaching deep into the past and far into the future. It becomes an infinity.[4]

Anatomy-as-Destiny Frightens Us All

Both men and women, I find, have a difficult time with the idea that our consciousness is biologically conditioned. Women are often fearful of any anatomical or biological differences between males and females being brought to the forefront again, lest these once again be used to put women down. Women fear questions such as: "Would you want a president having pre-menstrual tension during an international crisis?" "If women have menstrual problems, how can they hold responsible jobs?" So instead we have presidents whose male anxieties about proving their own toughness and masculinity impinge upon policy decisions every day of the month!

Should we pretend—in order to further female equality—that women do *not* menstruate? Should we instead dope them up with pills that make them function on the same unreal, unbodily and straight-out-with-caffeine way the male executive functions in our society? Should that then be called progress?

Men have a different sort of problem with the idea of biologically conditioned consciousness. Men truly can't imagine a situation in which they alone are not equipped to lead the world—if not as they are now, then improved with a little tinkering. If their sense of relationship with nature is a little off what it should be, then reform it; change "dominion-which-has-become-exploitation" to "responsible stewardship," and it will be all right for men to continue to rule the world. If man's present consciousness is not large enough, add some transcendental meditation, a few altered states of consciousness, a little therapy, a few more female roles, a concept of androgyny, lots of self-actualization, and you'll have a perfect male who is now *really* fit to rule the world.

Even the left brain and right brain research seems too good to be true. Just when our society begins to sense a need to turn away from overexposure to the stereotypically "rational" male ethos and for balance to turn to the supposedly "intuitive" female ethos, science discovers *both* are really in the male head. How fortuitous! Without such a discovery we might have thought women would actually have to have a major place in the seats of power in order to balance things. But now men can merely emancipate half their heads instead of emancipating women. How convenient, and men can continue to rule the world as before!

Men's confidence that they can or must "lead the world" is a confidence reinforced by their socialization but also intimately related to their lack of bodily limiting experiences. Men cannot seem to understand that this is their persistent problem they cannot get away from. Men's biologically conditioned consciousness is their Peter Pan shadow. It dogs them at every turn, because it is rooted in their own life experiences.

Woman, the Other Giver of Symbols

The solution? It cannot lie with the benign paternalism of the powerful—which the man (because he is a male and powerful) would always like to look to for solutions. Rather, I suspect, a balance between male and female perceptions needs to emerge. A balance which would be based upon recognition that humans come in two diverse forms. This more inclusive human experience of reality has been prevented by the powerful social conventions of patriarchal society from ever shaping for us a more adequate world view.

Thus the problem is not that men perceive like men—but that the male perception is not the entire human perception. What has been lacking is articulation of and attention to perceptions rooted in female experience.

*   *   *

I don't believe that I am alone in writing of childbirth as an ecstatic experience of my own body and one able to be shared with my husband. *For me as a woman my body taught me to surrender myself to the processes of life and to trust them.* Surrendering did not mean submission or passivity or giving up of myself or lack of activity. It *did* mean allying myself with the natural flow of energy. In that effort I discovered the inner dynamic of the process of life. "I" did not "have" a baby. She is not "my" daughter. My body became the instrument, the means by which the graceful, giftful dimension of life is experienced....

I found this experience caused me to reflect on the meaning of the word "creation"....I used to think of creation and the image of God as Creator as one who made, fashioned or shaped. I feel now, however, that the image of creation is best understood as being open to, sharing, participating, working with, surrendering to the movement of life, which will then give us more than we could ever gain by our own agency. This, ultimately, is the graceful dimension of existence, of relationships, of artistic creation, and I feel that through my body, specifically through the natural functioning of my female sexual structures, I have been given a perception of these graceful dimensions.[5] (Emphasis added.)

The very physical nature of a woman's being is no longer inarticulate as it was for so long. Penelope Washbourn is one of the women who are beginning to give expression to a new metaphysic: woman as open, woman as connected, woman as one who can trust the processes of life.

But the question now is whether we—especially males—can accept the giver of new symbols, new metaphors, and new modes of viewing reality *if* the giver is Woman. Can the male give up his old monopoly on the role of decisive gift-giver? Can he share with Woman the role of image-maker in the culture? Even beyond that, can Man find in himself the open hand to receive a new image to complement his own when the giver is The Other? Even if his life depends upon it?

13.

Moving with the
Natural Grain of Life

Now I must begin again. I must begin with a new woman, with the one who goes to the Nursing Home.

It is evening and I have the lonesome feeling that I am far from home, but I do not know where home is.

*   *   *

Here there is no support. There is nothing I can do but survive. The time is at the turning. Evening is turning into night. The arc of the sky is filled with great bands of sunset. Birds are flying high. It is a lonely time for me. I feel lost and far away from home. But where is home? I have never found it.

*   *   *

So after the supper had been cleared away, I stepped out into the night. My night. It was black night and the stars were my stars, I was alone with them. It was so still, the only sound was the tide coming, coming in, coming in. It was a pulse. It was there, it never stopped. It said be still and know that I am here. The timing of the pulse was the timing of my pulse. So I am the child of the tide.[1]

Living Lightly on the Earth

A child of the tide will be sensitive to the pulse of natural cycles and to the flow or lay of the land. We have few examples of this in our present way of operating. But what this would mean for our living with the sea and dunes and sandbars and shallow bay of the New Jersey Shore is described by the landscape architect Ian McHarg in *Design with Nature*.

> ...The sand dune is a very recent formation [geologically]. It will change its configuration in response to autumn hurricanes and winter storms and will sometimes be breached....The New Jersey Shore...is continuously involved in a contest with the sea; its shape is dynamic.[2]

118

McHarg points out that the relative stability of the dunes and the string of coastal islands they form is dependent for that stability upon vegetation—reeds, sea grasses, certain shrubs and trees—which anchor the sand against the actions of waves and wind. He then goes on to analyze from an ecologist's viewpoint what each of the several rows of dunes formed by the action of waves and wind provides for the shoreline's stability, what their tolerances and vulnerabilities are, and precisely how humans must design their human activities to fit within such natual tolerances—or upset that stability of the dunes.

> We now have the broad outlines of an ecological analysis and a planning prescription based upon this understanding. A spinal road could constitute a barrier dune and be located in the backdune area. It could contain all utilities, water, sewer, telephone and electricity and would be the guardian defense against backflooding. At the widest points of the backdune, settlement could be located in communities. Development would be excluded from the vulnerable, narrow sections of the sandbar. The bayshore [facing the mainland] would, in principle, be left inviolate. The beach [facing the ocean] would be available for the most intensive recreational use, but without building. Approaches to it would be by bridges [inland from the ocean beach] across the dunes, which would be prohibited to use. Limited development would be permitted in the trough, determined by groundwater withdrawals and the effect upon vegetation.[3]

McHarg points to Holland, which in order to reclaim land below sea level does adapt its human settlements to the shapes and needs of its shoreline.

> The dune grass, hero of Holland, is an astonishingly hardy plant, thriving in the most inhospitable of environments. Alas, it is incapable of surmounting the final crucial test of man. In the Netherlands, the vulnerability of dune grasses to trampling is so well understood, that dunes are denied to public access; only licensed naturalists are permitted to walk on them.... If you would have dunes protect you, and the dunes are stabilized by grasses, and these cannot tolerate man, then survival and the public interest is well served by protecting the grasses. But in New Jersey they are totally unprotected. Indeed nowhere along our entire eastern seaboard are they even recognized as valuable![4]

In everything—from farming to building human settlements—human activity must conform itself, McHarg says, to the "lay of the land" and its natural cycles and processes. *For ultimately human productivity can only be sustained over time by a partnership with natural productivity.*

The farmer is the prototype. He prospers only insofar as he understands the land and by his management maintains its bounty. So too with the man who builds. If he is perceptive to the processes of nature, to materials and to forms, his creations will be appropriate to the place; they will satisfy the needs of social process and shelter, be expressive and endure. As indeed they have, in the hill towns of Italy, the island architecture of Greece, the medieval communities of France and the Low Countries and, not least, the villages of England and New England.[5]

When the child of the tide can claim the natural processes as part of herself/himself, we will be sensitive out of kinship and caring, not out of "responsiblity" and "duty." We will be like sailors and those who design their boats and their sails, attentive to how the wind blows, how the waves move, and how the tides run, in order to know how best to sail *with* the boat, *with* the sails, and *with* the elements.

As a Hand Slips into a Glove

"Ecological reconnaissance" has been suggested as a practical way to make sure human developments fit appropriately within natural systems. Dr. Beatrice Willard, who made the suggestion, has had extensive experience as a field ecologist, in addition to serving in the Executive Office of the President on the prestigious three-member Council on Environmental Quality. She writes:

> I spent a day of ecological reconnaissance of the alpine tundra with the design engineer, locating for him within the route of a proposed high-tension line both the transient, unstable life-systems and the permanent, mature ones. By doing this the engineer was able to locate transmission-line towers so as to avoid the mature stands— some of which are several thousand years old, judging from the depth of soil accumulated. Without this knowledge, the engineer would have eradicated thousands of years of tundra development with a few hours work, for he had proposed a tower for the center of one of these old stands.

> So it is with all development. . . . With prior ecological investigation, design and development can be planned so as to maintain game migration routes, fisheries, winter grazing grounds, grass beds, striped bass spawning areas, zones of seismic activity, mature old stands of vegetation, marshes, woods, prairies, and other habitats for rare plants and animals. . . .[All this] can be done best and cheapest when a comprehensive plan is developed in the earliest stages. It is much more difficult, for example, to accomplish habitat rebuilding or restoration of a species' population after construction on the project has begun. But it may be relatively simple to work around a

segment of habitat which should be saved.... *Actions can harmonize with ecosystems, as a skilled hand slips adroitly, gently, smoothly into a glove, with little or no disruption of either the hand or the glove.*[6]

In the past, however, we have been too preoccupied with our anthropocentric pretensions to bother even to observe the way the natural systems worked. Although a few specialists may have studied these things, we have arranged our major and minor human systems across the grain of the way nature works. Our use of water to flush away human wastes is a classic example. Even a casual look at organic matter decaying to enrich the soil would have shown us that organic wastes should be returned to the earth to decay and enrich it. Yet we are now stuck with stupid arrangements and massive capital investments in flushing our toilets into sewers, rivers and oceans—and still further great investments in vast sewage treatment facilities to clean water which shouldn't have been dirtied in the first place. Meanwhile, back on the farm and in our gardens the soil is stripped of nutrients which never come back as wastes, and we restore the soil with chemical fertilizers made from precious (and also depleting) natural gas. This availability of artificial fertilizers has led farmers to using more than the crops can absorb; the cash crops never lack for fertilizer and grow like crazy, but the excess is washed—you guessed it—into rivers and lakes by rains, threatening our waters with a new hazard, "eutrophication" or so many nutrients that water grasses (like the cash crops) grow like crazy and clog our waterways, ponds and lakes.[7]

It is all very senseless and unperceptive of the natural grain of life. It tells us a great deal about the arrogant rationality of the human animal, that we created such arbitrary human systems without any attempt to fit them into the vast natural systems—*of which we are a part, even though we thought we were above.* The truth is that whether it is a sewerage system or an industrial production line, men have created arbitrary and linear systems in vast conceptual disregard of the fact that the world is based upon circular flows and functions in vast systems of recycling. The straight lines and single-mindedness of linear systems do not fit into such circles; they disrupt them.

Nature Magnifies Well-Designed Systems

Our task as architects of the future is to redesign and restructure our linear human systems until they are congruent with natural systems, until they do recycle. Beyond this we might even be clever enough, as Howard T. Odum suggests, to design human systems so well that we help natural systems work for us, thus magnifying our efforts.[8]

Let me illustrate this. I was in church one Sunday morning when the sun poured thorough a stained glass window in such a way that the whole window shimmered and danced with colors which had come alive in the power of the sun. The other stained glass windows in the church were dark and almost black. I suddenly realized that the stained glass windows were designed so that without the natural power of the sun they were nothing. But when the sun came through at just the right angle and time of day and year, the sun joined with that colored glass to do what no colored glass could do on its own. We must do this too. We must be humble enough and kindred enough with natural systems of which we are a part to design our human systems so responsively, so sensitively, that we do *with* nature what we cannot do alone—shine, shimmer and dance in a healthy symbiosis of those who together enjoy the goodness of creation.

John Todd and the New Alchemy Institute in Woods Hole, Massachusetts, have developed a number of such ways natural and human systems can work together. The waste of one part becomes food for another, and it all takes place in a naturally powered, symbiotically integrated and cascading and multiplying way.[9] John Todd describes how he first learned to do this:

It occurred to me that here I'd been in university since 1957, thirteen or fourteen years in academia—and many of these students had been in almost as long as I had—and we simply weren't trained in sensitive stewardship. We didn't know anything. Science hadn't trained us to be able to answer the most fundamental questions: How do you make that piece of earth sing, and how do you make it support those that live there? Degrees in agriculture, disease ethology, ecology...nothing!

So I decided we had to figure a way. I decided each student is going to study one component of this place. You're gonna do rocks, you're gonna do earthworms, you're gonna do grasses, you're gonna do herbs, you're gonna do snails, you're gonna do wind, you're gonna do sun, you're gonna do ferns...fourteen components. And there's two things you're gonna do before you pass this course: one is to find out what's here and in what abundance, and the second is you're gonna teach somebody else what you've learned.

Several months later...people were camping out, living in trees, stuff like that...and they grumbled like hell! Studying earthworms was not their idea of graduate school. But then they started to teach one another, and all of a sudden, like the scales falling from our eyes, a piece of land came alive. One of the students found a plant that only grows where there's water! So we dug down and found water! And it happened in a place where we could build a series of little dams like steps down the valley, and with the sun there, all of a sudden we had a driving wheel for the whole system. Another student found miner's lettuce, which meant we had a sort of balanced soil association, and the guy with the worms was able to collaborate. All of a sudden we had gardens, and the wind guy figured out a source of energy. And all of a sudden we were talking for the first time like we knew what we were talking about, even though we had just barely got the doors open! And here was this piece of land which was no longer an inhospitable enemy. Everywhere we were finding allies. Without knowing what was there, we never would have gotten the door open far enough to see what was inside. It was very heavy for me.

There has never been any doubt for me since that time that the way to go is to be whole. Know the sun, know the plants, know the soil, know the people, know the shelter...have them all interlaced, begin from there.[10]

The person who interviewed John Todd sums up the New Alchemy experience:

The essential requisite for the success of New Alchemy—and everyone here seems to sense it—is not money (though of course money is needed, or they will go under). It is this sense of a balanced interdependence with each other and with nature and an understanding of the delicacy of that balance. It is what John Todd calls the concept of interconnected webs. What New Alchemy provides is more than just hardware, more than just a solar-heated, wind-powered greenhouse/aquaculture complex that is inexpensive to construct, operates almost anywhere, and produces no-cost food—in itself a unique and important gift to the world—but a tangible way to use the environment constructively instead of destructively, a way to live in harmony with our own ecosystem, a way to use the sun and the wind and the elements to produce nourishing food. And *that* is alchemy.[11]

Fitting human life within natural cycles is not only for future new human settlements but it appears also to be the way to wiggle past critical environmental problems created by past patterns of human settlement or by natural fluctuations in climate and precipitation. Erik Eckholm and Lester Brown write in *Spreading Deserts: The Hand of Man* how—

In the desert, as elsewhere, planners have much to learn from the plants, animals, and cultures that have withstood centuries of extraordinarily adverse environmental conditions. If the ecological balance historically maintained by most nomadic groups was rather wretched, predicated as it was on high human death rates, these people used the life-defying desert remarkably resourcefully. In popular mythology, nomads are often pictured as aimless wanderers. But in fact, nomadic movements nearly always harmonize with the seasonal rhythm of climate and plant life. They are geared to permit animals to find adequate forage throughout the year and to permit the regrowth of grazing lands.

A return to an earlier historical age is no more desirable than likely.... Rudimentary modern medicine has trickled into the arid zones well ahead of advanced agricultural technology, helping push down death rates. Moreover, national boundaries now divide natural ecological zones artificially and restrict the traditional movements of nomadic groups, while the spread of sedentary agriculture further limits migrations.... Although many traditional nomadic practices are no longer viable, adopting some modernized version of the nomadic way of life may be the only way that those in the arid desert fringes can safely exploit these areas' protein-producing potential. Regional management schemes, in which clan leaders regulate grazing and migratory movements according to natural conditions and the advice of range specialists, represent one possibility.[12]

When the Earth Is Mythed as Female

As I write this, I am not at all sure male culture can muster the sensitivities necessary to do this fitting in. Let me tell you a curious story. Recently my husband and I were in Iceland for an international conference on the future of the global environment. A highlight of the bus tour of the capital city of Reykjavik was a visit to the studio of their eminent local sculptor Asmundur Sveinsson (whose sculpture of "Mother Earth" I described earlier). He has another statue "Music of the Sea," which is a woman's body, sitting down, wide open and exposed in the pelvis, with one leg back and one forward. She is leaning back, her head flung back, with one arm forward and out, and the other arm back. But she is laced with ropes that cut into her knees and breasts and are strung like a musical instrument to each of her hands. I as a woman winced in pain as I looked at that statue; I could feel the vagina exposed and the breasts hurting where the ropes laced through them.

When Matthias Johannessen was writing a book about Sveinsson, he asked the sculptor about this statue. "But it's a female figure," the sculptor replied, "I made her breasts like a boat. And her feet grow out of the wave which again turns into a thigh. It's all waves. And the hand is holding the strings. The music of the sea."[13] You can see here, quite unself-conscious in Asmundur Sveinsson, the deep equation of the woman and nature, the symbolization of this in the body of the woman, and the total lack of sensitivity to what is *done to* the body of the woman. So long as men consciously or unconsciously symbolized natural processes as female—and "female" means to them controlled and subordinated—then our fitting into nature will be delayed and distorted by the male need to control and subordinate.

Fascinated with the sculptor's lack of sensitivity to what was being done to the body of the woman in "Music of the Sea," I began using a postcard photograph of the statue as a litmus test or Rorschach test with some of our most perceptive male friends and colleagues. I made a startling discovery. Men do not identify with the body of that woman! Men do not sense her vaginal vulnerability in the pose of that statue, and (even more curious!) they do not feel the pain of those ropes laced into her breasts and knees.

I found this surprising. And chilling for the future of the earth. Eugene Bianchi's words come to mind about what happens between a woman and a man when he rapes her: "As a subhuman, her terror and pain call forth no empathy."[14] This is for me the predicament of the earth today. The male culture which is raping her does not identify (perhaps cannot identify) with the body of the earth which he myths as feminine. And because he cannot identify with it, he cannot seem to feel the mute pain.

Entering into Responsive Dialogue

Women are trained by their usual life-experience to be adept at non-verbal communication. The circumstances of their mothering force them to spend years responding to the needs of children, who even after they can speak often cannot identify what it is they need. As Tolstoy wrote somewhere, "The need is cry enough!" Have men ever such training in their life experiences? Can they understand the mute cry which has no words when nonetheless it speaks?

Jean Hersey in *The Shape of a Year* gives us in passing a number of examples of listening to non-verbal communications. She writes about the humans' need for water as well as that of plants during a drought:

It's all very well as a gardener to relate closely to nature and nature's ways, but it also has a slight drawback. When rain is needed I feel sort of parched, too. Of course, on the other hand, when rain does come, we gardeners have a tremendous sense of joy and relief, and can almost feel the earth absorbing water and roots replenishing themselves.

*   *   *

What the little wren has to tell when he perches on top of a garden post in the bright sunlight is beyond words. In some way he communicates his mood of joy and ecstasy and we quicken in response to fresh green everywhere, to a warming sun, and to merely being alive at the moment and listening to a small wren.

*   *   *

When you speed along in the car what do you know of the melody of a brook? Wind in meadow grass? The humming of bees in the clover? The subtle differences of bird songs, the crackle of someone's brush fire? As you walk each of your five senses seems to sharpen. There are the smells of the countryside which you never notice behind car windows, the fragrance of wild honeysuckle and the drifting scent of pear blossoms over someone's hedge.

*   *   *

You learn a lot about people when you take them walking in the woods. . . . Sometimes we start out speaking of everyday affairs, and after a few minutes the pauses in the conversation grow longer. The wood itself begins to speak and we fall silent. The sounds of a stream, of the wind in the tree-tops, the whir of a startled woodcock flying off, all seem more important than what we might say.[15]

To those who can so listen, so feel, so respond, living becomes a responsive dialogue. The child of the tide flows *with* the current of life just as the wind, flowing through my wind chime, produces the beauty of sound. May Sarton writes of this same responsive dialogue with the current of life in her existence as a person and poet:

I am more aware now than I was during his life of how much Quig's friendship, his very existence even apart from our own relationship, did to help me forge out the position of these last years about my work. It is good for a professional to be reminded that his professionalism is only a husk, that the real person must remain an amateur, a *lover* of the work. Whatever we do well is done spontaneously for its own sake, in just the way Quig suddenly decided that he had to get up to the schoolhouse room and paint, or, equally spontaneously, had to make muffins! I am, I think, more of a poet than I was before I knew him, if to be a poet means *allowing life to flow through one rather than forcing it to a mold the will has shaped;* if it means learning to let the day shape the work, not the work, the day, and so live toward essence as naturally as a bird or a flower.[16] (Emphasis added.)

14.

The Breaking Up of the Hierarchical Paradigm

This certain summer day is not only hot and humid, but it also has a peculiar and distinctive stillness, a kind of waiting quality, as if Nature is explaining how we are now at the top and soon we'll turn and move down the other side of the hill.

Did you ever watch the tide change? There is a similar moment of quiet when the water has run all the way out in a long slow sigh. For an instant of deep silence, Nature holds her breath and then inhales again. You feel a spark of inner quickening as you become aware of this hesitation that warns of such a significant change.[1]

The Turning of the Tide

There is a spark of inner quickening today that warns of significant change—of the turning of the tide. The dominant paradigm or picture in our minds of the world beyond our reach is turning. It is changing. And a whole new frame of mental reference is forming which emphasizes wholeness, connectedness and interdependence, and a different consciousness of self, others, human society and the natural world.

The theologian Kenneth Cauthen describes the dimensions of this change:

A new Gestalt is beginning to emerge. By this I mean that history is pregnant with a comprehensive way of perceiving, conceiving, and believing to which we are beckoned to help give birth. The new vision exists as a possibility arising out of the actualities of the present, but it lures us forward to actualize it in human thought, feeling, and action.

The evidences of this evolving world view are appearing in the natural sciences, in the social sciences, in psychology, and in philosophy. It is beginning to be articulated by physiologists, biologists, economists, ecologists, planners, systems analysts, anthropologists, political scientists, futurists, and visionaries....

The new vision centers in an intuitive perception of wholes, or organized unities. Key words are [w]holistic, unitary, organic, synergy, and synthesis. The focus of attention is on total systems, seen as a unity of dynamically interacting, mutually sustaining parts, which work together to support the functions and goals of the whole unit.[2]

Sometimes when the tide is changing, there is that peculiar and distinctive stillness and waiting, followed by the turn. Other times looking out across the water, you can see the tide change by the way the waves change. First here and then there, water movements reverse invisibly beneath the surface. It is then that you can, if you are looking, see the wind catch the water differently so that the waves look different where the tide has turned. I want to look with you now at some of the places in our society where the waves are looking different now, where the tide shows signs of having changed.

We referred earlier to biology and subatomic physics where the paradigm has already changed. Willis W. Harman in *An Incomplete Guide to the Future* points out that the winds of change continue to blow in science, as research into consciousness and into psychic phenomena such as telepathy, clairvoyance, precognition, and psychokinesis threaten to break open further old scientific beliefs which have declared such phenomena impossible.

The tide is also changing around the religious institutions of Western civilization. The human spirit is reaching out in a bewildering panorama of religious and semi-religious movements to reclaim our connection to a mysterious spirit-dimension of our selfhood which, in our excessive concern with rationality, has been lost. The turning of some to the charismatic movment, to the Jesus Freaks, and to the Moonies is powerful evidence of a quickening within or alongside of traditional Western Christianity. Others have turned to Zen, the Divine Light Mission, Transcendental Meditation, or other derivatives of traditional Eastern religions. Still others turn to newer religious movements such as Scientology or to self-realization movements such as Arica and est.

Process philosophy, systems analysis, and the women's movement—how different! Yet each is a Trojan horse now within the high walls and moated castles of hierarchical thinking and the old paradigm. To think or feel systemically is to perceive wholistically. To think interconnectedly is to re-knit the body of knowledge which has been divided into problem areas and academic disciplines of the various specialties. We will never be the same again when it becomes apparent what systemic (or non-hierarchical) perceptions arising from these movements mean for the university, for the church, and for the economic, sexual, political, technological, and household arrangements of society.

Our approach to problems and problem-solving will also never be the same again. Scientific reductionism—reducing a problem to its parts and then understanding those parts by specialization—will never again seem appropriate for all reality, and will become an important tool of limited usefulness. Our linear "one problem/one solution" thinking and our 1-2-3 outlines will be similarly humbled. All these are parts of a piecemeal way of approaching reality, and time has run out on that way of thinking.

But, you may ask, what if piece-by-piece is the only way the human mind can comprehend reality? What if we cannot grasp the interconnected realities of wholes? We will then know we have not ever grasped all of reality. We will then be more tentative about the adequacy of our proposed solutions. And when we shape our tools—our computers, our system dynamics studies and our systems analyses and whatever else we can dream up—our goals will be more modest. We will be content just to approximate a little better than before what we will now see as a complex web of relationships, alive, life-giving, and constantly changing.

The New Savoring of Diversity

We will come to a new appreciation of the wisdom, shrewdness, and intuitive system-perceptions of "little people" as we finally acknowledge the actual complexity we are attempting to live within. Women, children, minorities, the local cop, the bookkeeper, the salesperson, the elevator operator, all the people who with a part of their lives are cogs in some part of our vast complex systems—these people are often not highly trained. Their judgment has been shaped by limited but intensely immediate experience. They see things and understand things that never make it into supervisory reports or monthly statistics which, abstracted, go "to the top." Or into someone's financial control system which grinds everything down to the bottom line.[3]

What these sorts of people know about where they live and what affects what they do, they have learned outside the processes of super-rational socialization which constitute the central experience of those who achieve eminence in our society, our predominantly male elites. There is among non-elites a widely held perception (and skepticism) of specialist-knowledge, of experts themselves, and of those they report to who supposedly are "in charge." Eloise Maclay expresses this sort of perception—here in terms of psychiatrists and psychologists, but clearly the sentiment has obvious wider applicability:

> They,
> Psychiatrists,
> Psychologists,
> The experts,
> Keep reinventing the wheel.
> I just read where
> Studies show
> Gazing at water,
> Brooks, rivers, the sea,
> Is tranquilizing.
> Next thing you know
> They'll discover that crowds
> Make people nervous.
> The longer I live,
> The more it seems to me
> Life is a gigantic Easter egg hunt.
> We go running around like crazy,
> Hunting for brilliant truths
> You've hidden in plain sight.[4]

In the past we have only appreciated the brilliance of the "stars," the elites who were at the top of cultural pyramids. We are slowly learning to appreciate the sparkle and importance of a diversity of people and a diversity of standing points within human systems.

Frederick C. Thayer in his book *An End to Hierarchy! An End to Competition!* has identified how the hierarchical structuring of organizations has contributed to the devaluing of diversity in our culture. He points out that hierarchical organization is ultimately inefficient and destructive, as is economic competition. Why? Because he sees "alienation as the inexorable outcome of both." He argues for a wholistic and systemic understanding of organizations and society in which a diversity of people and a diversity of locations in a system all have contributions which are needed. Thayer urges a "new paradigm of mutually supportive interaction [that] will not require that individual contributions be evaluated, one against the other; *all* contributions will be valued."[5]

The devaluing of diversity is a seldom perceived problem of hierarchy. When difference is perceived and immediately rated as above or below in status or power, then that which is perceived as "below" is expected to give up its diversity (inferiority) and aspire to be like that which is superior. Even our American tradition of being the great "melting pot" implied that the diversity coming into the United States would become Americanized. And at the top of that system was the WASP—the white, Anglo-Saxon Protestant who was the epitome of what it means to be straight/white/male. It was not a diversity game at all but a game of conformity in which the social tyranny of those at the top was subtly but firmly established, if not always by wealth and power, then by status.

The Tyranny of Norms

The dynamics by which hierarchies oppress and alienate has been explored further in a book about the hierarchies of male/female, white/black, and heterosexual ("straight")/homosexual ("gay") edited by Glenn R. Bucher. *Straight/White/Male* presents, among other things, the uses of social norms and the ways in which social difference become the occasion for social hierarchies of status, power and oppression. It is a book about the tyranny of norms.

Social norms are the standards establishing which end of the social ladder is up. Some people embody these standards and find them natural expressions of who they are. For the rest those standards are that by which they are judged to be different than the norm and hence inferior. They "are not up to the norm." A social norm has power to oppress only because it is an expression of a social hierarchy or pyramid of status or power. The standards of status or power (and hence of oppression) may be clearly articulated (as in apartheid or in Jim Crow laws). Or they may be intuited as pervasive and seemingly universal social conventions (as in people's responses to Eliza Doolittle's perceived social status in *My Fair Lady*—responses which changed totally as Eliza, with Professor Higgins' help, learned to speak "better" English).

"Sociologically speaking," Glenn Bucher writes, "to be the oppressor is to be the social norm and reference point against which every definition of abnormality is judged." He goes on to point out that "Whiteness, maleness, and heterosexuality are presumed to be *the human criteria* against which all others are measured."[6] He illustrates with the hierarchy in the small towns of America:

> Against this model [of independent middle-class Protestant males] all other social creatures are evaluated. Those who are not middle-class; who do not participate in respectable social institutions; who are not products of a "stable" home; who cannot claim they are

"independent middle-class persons verbally living out Protestant ideals in the small towns of America," are destined to be social exceptions.

To be the oppressor, then, means to be the *human* social norm. It is to have social prejudice, society's mores, and public morality tilted in one's direction. It is not to worry about respectability or respect. It is to be comfortable. It is to be familiar with social expectations. It could not be otherwise, given that straight white males also determine both the social rules and the punishments for those who fail to conform.[7]

Such social "ratings" of people become additionally expressed in what they can get paid for their "worth" and their work. "Whether we speak of blacks in cotton fields (or their contemporary equivalents), women qua mothers in the home whose labor is free, or homosexuals discriminated against vocationally due to sexual preference," writes Bucher, "the conclusion is verifiable: straight white males perpetuate these economic arrangements, if in no other way, by their tacit approval of the economic benefits thereby procured for themselves. To be the oppressor is to be master of the 'American plantation.' A glance at the constituency of any corporate board, or the roster of America's chief corporate administrative officers, puts to rest any doubt."[8]

Within such a "looking upward" society the need to become other than oneself has devastating psychological consequences. Consider the black experience:

White wealth, white beauty, white culture were not only dominant but the standards by which all else was judged. Thus, nappy hair, the broad nose, the thick lips of the black person, being the antithesis of white characteristics, were ugly. Some blacks—at the time the vast majority of blacks—underwent much physical pain in a futile attempt, not to be *like* white people but to *be* white. And, as this is a physical impossibility, a certain psychopathology developed in which the black person became a non-person. Franz Fanon describes it this way: "When the Negro makes contact with the white world, a certain sensitizing action takes place. If his psychic structure is weak, one observes a collapse of the ego. The black man stops behaving as an *actional* person. The goal of his behavior will be The Other (in the guise of the white man), for The Other alone can give him worth."[9]

But there is a sense in which norms tyrannize all, and in which even those perceived from below to be oppressors are themselves oppressed. It is the oppression of a socialization which demands that the character and personality of particular individual males be narrowed to conform to the stereotype being approved and rewarded.

It is the common experience of men to be socialized into the competitive, aggressive, individualistic attitudes necessary to build a career in a society that considers those character traits to be superior. Furthermore, it is the collective experience of males to be psychologically dependent upon their career success for satisfaction and a positive self-image.[10]

*   *   *

The worth of a male is measured by self and others on the basis of success standards related to these aspects of his life. Economic power, personal wealth, political power, professional status, straight sexual prowess, and control over the family are indices of normative masculinity.[11]

The tyranny of this straight, white male norm has only very recently been questioned by the movements of "Black Is Beautiful," ethnicity, gayness and sisterhood.

Over the past ten years, the cultural hegemony dominating America has begun to erode as different segments of the population have come to see that America has been exclusively defined according to the needs and desires of a ruling elite of white, middle-aged, male heterosexuals. In turn blacks, the young, women, and homosexuals have challenged this hegemony and as a result America is more fragmented, more divided, and yet freer than ever before in its history.[12]

The Decline of the Power of the Norm

An analysis of TV programming from 1960 to 1975 that I did several years ago[13] provides an interesting mirror in which to view the erosion of this cultural hegemony. When we look at TV historically, we see the early programs were all centered around exceptional individuals—super comics such as Bob Hope, Red Skelton, Jack Benny, super singers such as Perry Como, Bing Crosby, Frank Sinatra, super Western heroes as in "Gunsmoke" or "Bonanza," super war heroes as in "Twelve O'Clock High," super sleuths as in "Perry Mason" and "Bat Man," super knowledge as in "The $64,000 Question," even super dogs like "Lassie."

Underlying the choice of all these programs was the assumption that the main character of a TV program was an outstanding person or persons in some way normative for the rest of society to admire. In this period almost all the main characters were white males (with the notable exception of Lucille Ball in "I Love Lucy"). When families were the focus of a situation comedy, as in "I Love Lucy," "Leave It to Beaver," "Ozzie and Harriet," "The Dick Van Dyke

Show," and that classic "Father Knows Best," the family was always "typical"—white, middle-class, Mother and Father both in residence, usually two children, and the father always employed in a secure white-collar job such as an insurance salesman, lawyer, or doctor. About the only exception in that period was "The Andy Griffith Show," which had a father alone raising a son with the assistance of Aunt Bea, who kept house for them. "Andy Griffith" was also different in being set in a small town in the South at a time when most family shows were suburban.

In the late 1960s the family situation comedy moved into a transitional phase with a burst of new shows which did not portray the usual "normative" family—"My Three Sons," "Family Affair," "The Partridge Family," "Julia," "The Courtship of Eddy's Father," and "The Brady Bunch." With the advent of these family shows, all the children in the viewing public who were living in so-called "broken homes" could now feel they were no longer odd or different from the norm, because the spectrum of what was "normal" had widened to include many different ways of living in families, and the settings had widened from suburban to urban high-rise and even in "Three for the Road" to a mobile home.

Women as main characters suddenly become numerous on the television screen in the early 1970s—first with "That Girl" and "Mary Tyler Moore" (both career women, unmarried), followed by "Rhoda" (married but the star), "Phyllis" (widowed), "Fay" (divorced woman), "Maude" (middle-aged, twice-divorced), "Policewoman" (white, sexy, competent), and "Christie Love" (black, sexy, competent).

This same period saw the rise of the black hero as in countless "shoot 'em up" shows—"Mission Impossible," "I Spy," "Mod Squad," "Ironside," "The Rookies," "SWAT"—competent and courageous black males became part of integrated teams. Similarly on children's television "Sesame Street" and "The Electric Company" made city streets and black faces commonplace in a way that "Captain Kangaroo" had not done for an earlier generation of children.

But could television go lower-class? And could it portray those who were handicapped physically or whose competencies were not heroic but human? Into the world of the fast-moving and agile detective came "Ironside," the cripple, doing his detecting from a wheelchair and letting his staff do the nabbing. Soon to follow was "Longstreet," an insurance investigator who is blind but manages to be efficient in his own way. "Harry O" stands out as a private eye because he alone, anticipating the energy crisis, does not give chase in sleek automobiles but rides the common bus!

There has always been an economic dimension to television heroics. Archie Bunker in "All in the Family" was perhaps the break-through for the class barrier. For a long time the jobs of the main character on TV were always middle-class or above. But Archie works on a loading dock, lives in a smaller-scale non-suburban house, and feels like "a little guy who gets screwed by those big guys." "Sanford and Sons," "Chico and the Man," and "Arnie" take us into the lives of a junkman, a garage mechanic, and a foreman of the loading dock who has just taken the next step up.

So if we look at television as a mirror of our culture, what do we see has happened to the norm? The name of the game is not "rightness" any more, or "do you match the unattainable image of the hero?" The image has become broad enough to include almost all of us, black and white, Jewish and Puerto-Rican and Italian, whole and handicapped, young and middle-aged and elderly, female as well as male, bigoted as well as liberal.

The name of the game is now "people"—and people are diverse. The message is becoming clear on television, "I'm OK, you're OK." Whether crippled like Ironside, bigoted like Archie, abrasive like Maude, we can still identify with you, for what is being legitimized by television before our very eyes is *a new image of human diversity* and how precious, how fallible, how flawed, yet how okay it is.

Hierarchy Expressed in Law

Hierarchical thinking has embodied a refusal to receive the diversity of creation as enrichment and has perceived it instead as a threat. It is not surprising, then, that the ethical and legal systems evolved within hierarchical social systems have been structured not only to safeguard the position of those "above" but also to create limbos of legal "non-being" for what is defined by the hierarchy as "below" or "beyond legal rights."

Women, until they were no longer the property of men, had no legal rights of their own. Slaves had no legal rights; like women and children and animals and plants and land, slaves were the property of men, who were the only locus of legal rights. While animals today are not always considered property except when bought and sold, animals have no legal rights which could prevent their being hunted, trapped, used for research, starved to make them "eager eaters" for television commercials, and otherwise abused in ways that make you want to cry out. *Man Kind?* asks Cleveland Amory in his haunting book with the subtitle, "Our Incredible War on Wildlife."[14]

Peter Singer has written a book called *Animal Liberation: A New Ethics for Our Treatment of Animals.*[15] Singer coins the word "speciesism" to refer to "an attitude, often unconscious, that considers species other than our own to be without consciousness, feelings, or rights, existing only to be used for the convenience of the master species."[16] Singer contends that speciesism is as dangerous and insidious as racism and sexism because "it allows us to exploit, torture and kill other animals without feeling guilty."[17]

Carl Sagan also raises the question of animal rights very strongly in his book about the evolution of human intelligence:

> The cognitive abilities of chimpanzees force us, I think, to raise searching questions about the boundaries of the community of beings to which special ethical considerations are due....
>
> *   *   *
>
> If chimpanzees have consciousness, if they are capable of abstractions, do they not have what until now has been described as "human rights"? How smart does a chimpanzee have to be before killing him constitutes murder? What further properties must he show before religious missionaries must consider him worthy of attempts at conversion?
>
> I recently was escorted through a large primate research laboratory by its director. We approached a long corridor lined, to the vanishing point as in a perspective drawing, with caged chimpanzees. They were one, two or three to a cage, and I am sure the accommodations were exemplary as far as such institutions (or for that matter traditional zoos) go. As we approached the nearest cage, its two inmates bared their teeth and with incredible accuracy let fly great sweeping arcs of spittle, fairly drenching the lightweight suit of the facility's director. They then uttered a staccato of short shrieks, which echoed down the corridor to be repeated and amplified by other caged chimps, who had certainly not seen us, until the corridor fairly shook with the screeching and banging and rattling of bars....
>
> I was powerfully reminded of those American motion pictures of the 1930s and 40s, set in some vast and dehumanized state or federal penitentiary, in which the prisoners banged their eating utensils against the bars at the appearance of the tyrannical warden. These chimps are healthy and well-fed. If they are "only" animals, if they are beasts which abstract not, then my comparison is a piece of sentimental foolishness. But chimpanzees *can* abstract. Like other mammals, they are capable of strong emotions. They have certainly committed no crimes. I do not claim to have the answer, but I think it is certainly worthwhile to raise the question: Why, exactly, all over the civilized world, in virtually every major city, are apes in prison?[18]

Theodore S. Meth is a lawyer who teaches the only course in the country on animals and the law.[19] Meth raises some fascinating questions:

> Koko is a young female gorilla with a vocabulary and intelligence of a five-year-old child. Through sign-language, she converses with people and makes up new words when she doesn't have the exact word she wants. She talks to herself when she plays with her dolls. She is aware of herself. She probably reasons and feels very much as we do.
>
> * * *
>
> We are looking at a legal marvel, what I have called an "animal person."
>
> * * *
>
> The ability to use language has long been considered the characteristic that distinguishes man from animals. But what about Koko, the gorilla who "talks" in sign language? Have Koko and other trained primates crossed a legal dividing line [opening up a whole new legal era]?[20]

The Legal "Never-Never Land" of Children

Children today in our hierarchical society and legal system are viewed as "belonging" to their parents. This gives parents legal rights over their children which are nearly absolute and thus frightening in their implications. For example, in most states parents can commit their children to mental institutions without the child having any legal right to a lawyer, a hearing, or a chance to tell their side of the story.[21] Doctors who become aware of a pattern of injuries to a child which suggest child-abuse find it difficult to intervene; there is a strong tradition in our hierarchical culture which—apart from a few very general guidelines about child labor and required school attendance—presumes that parents have a right to raise their children in their formative years as the parents see fit. This is what it means for a child to be legally a "minor."

We are just beginning to take the lid off the problem of child-abuse and the related problems of wife-beating and rape, and admit to ourselves the prevalence and seriousness of these problems. Elizabeth Janeway has pointed out in "The Weak Are the Second Sex"[22] that men who perceive themselves to be powerless within our hierarchically structured economic and social systems, comfort themselves that they are at least "above women." I would make an analogy with the psychological needs of poor whites in the South who have tried to keep the black man "in his place" below them: men who feel economically impotent feel a need to "reign in power at home." Sometimes that power takes the form of hitting and physically abusing wife and children. Mothers too can feel impotent—and take out their feelings in physical abuse of their children.

We have laughed about the man who comes home from work and shouts at his wife, who in turn hits the child, who in turn kicks the cat or dog. Hierarchical systems channel frustrations and violence from above toward those below. Hierarchical thinking and legal systems legitimate the "exporting" of such stresses to those who are lower down in the pecking order.

The reality of widespread child-abuse as well as the selling of children by parents into child pornography are flagrant examples of the abuses of parenthood. These practices rest squarely upon the hierarchical presumption that adults "own" their children and are equipped to be "responsible stewards" of their children's lives.

But there are changes in the wind. Those "below" are becoming empowered, and they are challenging the ugly realities of physical abuse, incest, rape, and lynching, which constitute the violence (and threats of violence) that have held them in their place. Feminists are organizing to assist victims of wife-beating and rape. The culture-at-large is becoming more concerned about violent crimes such as rape and "in-house" exploitations such as incest and child-abuse.

Concern for the legal rights of children is building as more people perceive that the system as it is now legally structured gives children very few rights. It does this because our legal system conceptualizes children as having no rights but always being in the custody of those who do have rights—adults or society-as-parent. In the extremely important case *In Re. Gault* 387 U.S. 1 (1967), the U.S. Supreme Court gave to children for the first time certain due process rights heretofore residing only in adults. It held that in legal actions in which children were threatened with removal from their family to an institutional setting, they had the right to notice, to legal counsel, to cross-examine, and Fifth Amendment protection against self-incrimination.

The Exercise of Paternalism

If this is the ethical and legal standing of women, children and animals, what of nature itself? Aldo Leopold wistfully comments in his *Sand County Almanac* that ethical systems have never been extended from the human to the natural.

> When god-like Odysseus returned from the wars in Troy, he hanged all on one rope a dozen slave-girls of his household whom he suspected of misbehavior during his absence.
>
> This hanging involved no question of propriety. The girls were property. The disposal of property was then, as now, a matter of expediency, not of right and wrong. . . . The ethical structure of that day covered wives, but had not yet been extended to human chattels. During the three thousand years which have since elapsed, ethical criteria have been extended to many fields of conduct, with corresponding shrinkages in those judged by expediency only. . . .
>
> There is as yet no ethic dealing with man's relationship to land and to the animals and plants which grow upon it. Land, like Odysseus' slave-girls, is still property.[23]

Leopold seems to visualize the extension of ethics in horizontal terms—as in an ever-widening circle of light. But as any black will tell you, the movement from "property" to "peer" is upward, and the need to "move up" is totally derivative from the hierarchical paradigm that dominates our collective consciousness. You can see this hierarchical paradigm clearly in these passages from *Ecology and Human Liberation*, a book written for the World Council of Churches by Christian theologian Thomas Derr.

> No doubt about it, the Bible does say plainly that it is in the charter for man's existence that he should have "dominion" over and "subdue" the earth and all its other creatures. . . . The command comes only to man made "in the image of God." At the apex of creation, he is set in the Garden. . . . But the *original* placement of man above nature is not in error ecologically. . . .
>
> *   *   *
>
> It is the distinction from nature, the acceptance of dominion, that makes us human. We rise out of nature. The word we use for this process of human ascent is *civilization*. . . . Without his "spirit," he would be reduced to the level of the beasts. . . . [24]

Thomas Derr would be upset with the possibility of extending ethics or rights to nature, because he goes on to say:

> The principal intention of ecological revisionism in theology is to establish a value for nature independent of man and of such intensity that man may "love" it or hold it in "reverence". . . . Yet the revisionists argue that ecological destruction is wrong because it violates the earth itself, with its own intrinsic rights—not because such destruction makes it impossible for the divine-human drama to go on, and renders the lot of the masses miserable. But these latter points are more typical of Biblical concerns, rather more important than defending the intrinsic rights of nature.[25]

It is interesting to see this same abhorrence for the rights of nature expressed by Passmore in his classic, *Man's Responsibility for Nature.*

> One of my colleagues, an ardent preservationist, condemns me as a "human chauvinist." What he means is that in my ethical arguments, I treat human interests as paramount.... *The supposition that anything but a human being has "rights" is, or so I have suggested, quite untenable.*[26] (Emphasis added.)

The attitudes of Derr and Passmore toward intrinsic rights for nature reinforce my personal suspicion of interpretations of the environmental ethic as "reponsible stewardship." That concept is paternalistic, clothed still in hierarchical categories, and subtly related to such old ideas as "enlightened slave owners" and "the white man's burden." "To be graciously responsible for that which is below us" is not really our situation amid the interconnections of spaceship earth. Yet it is widely touted as an acceptable version of the environmental ethic and as the correct Judeo-Christian interpretation of that Genesis 1:26 text about "dominion."

Just as women did not wish to be the property of even "responsible husbands," and slaves did not wish to be owned by even the most enlightened slave owners, so too the earth will not flourish as the "property" of even responsible stewardship wielded from "above." Power corrupts, and self-interest always motivates those "above" to the detriment of those "below." Great is the power of human rationalization to justify such self-interest and to make it appear to be "responsible."

From Legal Limbo to Legal Standing

Just as women, children, gays, blacks, Chicanos, and the poor of the earth are reaching out from their hierarchical oblivion for their rights, some are also beginning to assert the claim of trees and animals and nature itself to intrinsic rights. That natural objects should have legal rights has been argued by Christopher D. Stone in an essay "Should Trees Have Standing?"[27] which appeared in late 1972 in the *Southern California Law Review.* This line of argument was almost immediately picked up by the U.S. Supreme Court in its minority opinions in the controvertial *Mineral King-Disney-Sierra Club* (4-3) decision.

Stone argues that natural objects should be accorded the three aspects of legal privileges which go with being a holder of legal rights: (1) the right to initiate legal action at *its own behest*; (2) the court, in determining the granting of legal relief, must take *injury to it* into account; and (3) legal relief must run to the *benefit of it*.[28]

Stone points out that corporations have legal standing. (I would add the obvious—that corporations have this legal standing only because a legal system dominated by white males decided they really needed corporations to have this legal standing.) And, like natural objects, corporations are not human. Corporations are abstractions and belong to a whole class of inanimate right-holders—trusts, corporations, joint ventures, municipalities, ships, and nation-states, to name a few—which Stone points out "people" the world of the lawyer.[29]

Because corporations and all these other inanimate human creations have rights, Stone sees no inherent legal reason for denying legal standing to natural objects. Though mute, natural objects are better able to communicate their needs than corporations.

> ...Natural objects *can* communicate their wants (needs) to us, and in ways that are not terribly ambiguous. I am sure I can judge with more certainty and meaningfulness whether and when my lawn wants (needs) water, than the Attorney General can judge whether and when the United States wants (needs) to take an appeal from an adverse judgment by a lower court.

> The lawn tells me that it wants water by a certain dryness of the blades and soil—immediately obvious to the touch—the appearance of bald spots, yellowing, and a lack of springiness after being walked on; how does "the United States" communicate to the Attorney General? For similar reasons, the guardian-attorney for a smog-endangered stand of pines could venture with more confidence that his client wants the smog stopped, than the directors of a corporation can assert that "the corporation" wants dividends declared. We make decisions on behalf of, and in the purported interests of, others every day; these "others" are often creatures whose wants are far less verifiable, and even far more metaphysical in conception, than the wants of rivers, trees, and land.[30]

It is fascinating to me that as Stone explores what has in the past made the extension of legal rights to oppressed minorities "unthinkable," he alludes to the presence of hierarchical thinking without ever explicitly labeling it as such.

> Throughout legal history, each successive extension of rights to some new entity has been, theretofore, a bit unthinkable. We are inclined to suppose the rightlessness of rightless "things" to be a decree of Nature, not a legal convention acting in support of some status quo. It is thus that we defer considering the choices involved in all their moral, social, and economic dimensions.

And so the United States Supreme Court could straight-facedly tell us in *Dred Scott* that Blacks had been denied the rights of citizenship "as a subordinate and inferior class of beings, who had been subjugated by the dominant race...." In the nineteenth century, the highest court in California explained that Chinese had not the right to testify against white men in criminal matters because they were "a race of people whom nature has marked as inferior, and who are incapable of progress or intellectual development beyond a certain point...between whom and ourselves nature has placed an impassable difference." The popular conception of the Jew in the 13th Century contributed to a law which treated them as "men *ferae naturae,* protected by a quasi-forest law. Like the roe and the deer, they form an order apart".....

The fact is, that each time there is a movement to confer rights onto some new "entity," the proposal is bound to sound odd or frightening or laughable. This is partly because until the rightless thing receives its rights, we cannot see it as anything but a *thing* for the use of "us"—those who are holding rights at the time.[31]

A New Season

A new season is blowing up the valley, drifting over the hills, rising up from a cooling earth, a new season with its challenges, its changes, its excitements, and its own particular rhythms and miracles.[32]

A new season of consciousness is indeed blowing up the valley. There are people seriously talking about plants having feelings, about talking to plants, about communicating with the Devas (spirits of plant forms) as in the Findhorn gardens.[33] Ten years ago no one could have sold anyone a Pet Rock, not to mention sold tens of thousands at a price of five dollars each! Research on the dolphin language is taking place with the serious hope that someday we may talk back and forth with another species. Research with primates using sign-language and computer-language has already made that possible with the species closest to us. Our culture is beginning to take seriously the notion that consciousness is not solely a human attribute.

The opening up of consciousness to new ways of responding to life builds momentum as experiences multiply. New perceptions are reinforced while some of our old ones crumble. It is a dynamic which tears off old blinders, dynamites old roles, undermines old stereotypes, and finally leads through a long tunnel of mind-blowing experiences to new psychic space. Listen to Jean Hersey describe such an experience.

Recently Bob and I went to a lecture at which we learned a wonderfully interesting discipline. You take five minutes a day and look at any object—a paper clip, pencil, leaf, silver fork, flower—any object at all. For the whole five minutes you must keep your attention on the object in your hand. First you are supposed to see it physically, really observe it. Then you travel with it.... You can go forward or backward [in time], but *you must stay with the object....*

*   *   *

...I took up a small piece of jade that I had picked up some years ago on a beach near Big Sur, California. Holding it in my hand a while, I remembered reading somewhere that God sleeps in stones, stirs in vegetables, wakes in animals, and moves through Man. What a potential there was in that stone in my palm!

I began to look at it, study its tear-drop shape and color variations, and to be aware of its pleasant smoothness. It appeared to be a solid stone; but in the light of what we know today, I told myself, it is really made of separate atoms with spaces between each and if I were small enough, I could pass through it. In a kind of reverie, I imagined the stone growing larger and larger and myself smaller until I could enter it. Then I passed easily among the atoms that formed tall green corridors like a great forest and I was aware of a rhythmic swaying around me.

I don't know how long I was there, but after a while I was back in our living room with a small piece of jade in my hand, sun streaming in the window—and it was time to go for the mail.

*   *   *

It taught me that normally I don't half see what I look at. I began looking at everything differently and really seeing the blanket as I made the bed, the texture of the sock I darned, the carrot I peeled. A thrilling world opened up around me in the little daily things that I handled and had not really appreciated.[34]

The changing of consciousness is like the ice breaking up after a long winter. This particular changing of consciousness is akin to the breakup of feudalism at the end of the Middle Ages, as old patterns of life and thought split apart and crumble away. New constellations of perception slowly formed, and out of them was born our modern world—the structures of political, economic and social life we call our own. So too today, old patterns are crumbling, and out of the ruins will emerge new institutions built upon totally new ways of perceiving and living in our world. History is at a turning point.

In such a time of transition, we cannot see clearly where the changes lead. We can only sense the loss of momentum in one direction and feel the surging newness in another, impatient to be born. It is a time to take a mental breath and let go.

15.

We Must Re-Myth Genesis

This hour of the day is so incredibly beautiful that I am filled with wonder. The late afternoon sun, still vigorous with warmth but mellow with diminishing, is flooding our deck and beach and small cove with lustrous sidelighting. Like a Vermeer painting, it catches the white sides of the moored boats, making them gleam like translucent ivory. The sun goes in for a moment. I look up and see sheaths of lighted vapor shooting up out of the cloud like streaks of ethereal power. The sun comes back, and the sea is lit to an incredible aqua blue which shines back at me with a liquid sheen.

I have always wanted to paint this hour and the evening time which follows it—to attempt to capture, as the French impressionists did, the wondrous glories of light in nature. When my children were small and constantly demanding and interrupting at this hour, it seemed to me the very first thing I would do with post-motherhood leisure would be to try to paint this. But I never have, perhaps because I fear the failure to capture such an elusive essence. Instead I find I want simply to experience it deeply, over and over.

And so I sit on my deck and look out. And I feel and see and notice everything—the small white butterflies playing in twos and threesomes over the beach roses, the gulls flying in lazy swoops over their island, the different way each evening takes shape as the pale blue sky gradually deepens until it almost matches the deepening blue-purple of the water, striated now with a thousand ripple lines which catch the sun and cast their own tiny shadows. Each evening is different, unique, special. The sun and the earth, the wind and the water and the birds—each is a glorious gift of life to me...if I participate,...if I am still,...if I can listen and receive and wonder and worship.

The Covenant in Creation

We have never understood that there is a covenant in creation itself. God reaches out to us in creation, births us into being,

144

surrounds us with the splendors of sensual life in a sensuous universe, and pledges faithfulness to us in the steadiness of the seasons and in the bounty of food for eyes, mind, ears and stomachs. God's gift to us *is* this life, this world, this creation. God's pledge to us is the constancy of the pulse of life in creation itself.

The poet laureate of South Carolina, Archibald Rutledge, has this sense of the creation as the foundational communication from God.

> The more I thought about this, the more it appeared that Creation supplies us with only two kinds of things: necessities and extras. Sunlight, air, water, food, shelter—these are among the bare necessities. With them we can exist. But moonlight and starlight are distinctly extras; so are music, the perfumes, flowers. The wind is perhaps a necessity; but the song that it croons through the morning pines is a different thing.
>
> *   *   *
>
> I stood recently on the shores of a mountain lake at sundown after a heavy rain, and watched for an hour the magnificence of the west; the huge clouds smoldering, the long lanes of emerald light between them, then isolated clouds like red roses climbing up some oriel window of the sky, the deep refulgence behind it all. Superb as it was, momently it changed, so that I saw in reality a score of sunsets. I looked across the lonely, limpid lake, past the dark forest, far into the heart of the flaming, fading skies....
>
> Neither a day-dawning nor a sunset (with all its attendant beauty) is really a necessity. It is one of life's extras. It is a visit to an incomparable art gallery; and no one has to pay any admission fee.
>
> *   *   *
>
> Almost the whole complex and wonderful matter of color in the world seems an extra. The color of the sky might have been a dingy gray, or a painful yellow, or a plum-colored purple. But it is sapphire. And my philosophy makes me believe that such a color for the sky is by no means the result of mere chance. Granted that it is the result of the operation of certain laws, forces, and conditions; yet behind it all, back of the realized dream, is the mighty intelligence of the Creator, the vast amplitude of the dreamer's comprehension....
>
> *   *   *
>
> ...I went one day into the forest to try to escape from a grief that had come to me.... All about me were the rejoicing looks of the flowers, and the shining hush and loveliness of dew-hung ferns and bushes, and the gentle, pure passion of the sunlight. And music there was from myriads of sources: gossamer lyrics from bees; the laughter of a little stream jesting with the roots of a mighty pine.... God seemed very near to me in that wood.... I saw there both life and death—in the green leaves and the brown, in the standing trees and the fallen.[1]

Rutledge tells here of the renewal of his sense of the constancy of the pulse of life in creation: "Passing from a state of keenest grief I came to one of quiet reconcilement—to the profound conviction that, living or dying, God will take care of us."[2]

The Covenant Set apart from Creation

The covenant in creation has never been properly understood. Instead, the covenant has always been construed as something apart from creation. Even though the Genesis myth pronounced the goodness of all of creation, Judeo-Christian religion never saw that in the creation of the world there had been a covenant given. Instead the ancient Hebrew made another covenant with God and made circumcision its sign and seal (Gen. 17:1-14). It was that covenant-pledge (circumcision) that constituted them as God's people.

This covenant religion, with its relation to a transcendent moral God, was sharply distinguished by all of Abraham's heirs from the Baal worship of the female fertility cults that flourished in neighboring regions of Canaan in the first millenium of their existence as a people. Yet in a strange way the ancient Hebrews had produced their own version, a male fertility cult, in which the central cultic act defining membership in the religion and tracing the descent of the bloodline focused upon the circumcised male phallus!

Within the dimensions of the biblical covenant, nature became a backdrop. It was a carpet and a stage-setting upon which the drama of salvation was being played out between sinful man and the transcendent God. Nature became in that perception of things a non-category. When nature was not completely ignored in theological discussion, it became a foil against which to display the human and honor that part of creation which was inward, spiritual, and "supernatural."

What had been completely overlooked was that God long ago had made a fundamental, initial and sustaining covenant with all of creation. Through the millenia God has been continually loyal to this covenant with an ongoing renewal of the seasons, the generations, and of creation itself. Because we missed seeing all that, we have not seen "honoring creation" as our side of the covenant.

Honoring the Diversity God Has Created

What God created was and is diverse. And complex. So the covenant is not just between us and God. Nor is it just between a few of the parts of what God has created and their Creator. The covenant, like the creation, goes in many directions. It is a covenant connecting, supporting and shaping all that in the intricate creation web sustains what has been made and recycles what is being reused and renewed.

To honor the convenant means to honor not only the Creator but to honor all those sustaining and renewing relationships. The poet Phyllis McGinley pointed to this in her poem on the occasion of a Phi Beta Kappa dinner. Such occasions usually honor excellence, but "In Praise of Diversity" directs praise and honor toward the entire covenant—toward all that the fantastically inventive mind of God has birthed into being.

> Since this ingenious earth began
>   To shape itself from fire and rubble;
> Since God invented man, and man
>   At once fell to, inventing trouble,
> One virtue, one subversive grace
> Has chiefly vexed the human race.
>
> One whimsical beatitude,
>   Concocted for his gain and glory,
> Has man most stoutly misconstrued
>   Of all the primal category—
> Counting no blessing, but a flaw,
> That Difference is the mortal law.
>
> Adam, perhaps, while toiling late,
>   With life a book still strange to read in,
> Saw his new world, how variegate,
>   And mourned, "It was not so in Eden,"
> Confusing thus from the beginning
> Unlikeness with original sinning.
>
> And still the sons of Adam's clay
>   Labor in person or by proxy
> At altering to a common way
>   The planet's holy heterodoxy.
> Till now, so dogged is the breed,
> Almost it seems that they succeed
>   *   *   *
>   . . . Yet who would dare
>   Deny that nature planned it other,
> When every freckled thrush can wear
>   A dapple various from his brother,
> When each pale snowflake in the storm
> Is false to some imagined norm?
>
> Recalling then what surely was
>   The earliest bounty of Creation:
> That not a blade among the grass
>   But flaunts its difference with elation,
> Let us devoutly take no blame
> If similar does not mean the same.

> And grateful for the wit to see
> Prospects through doors we cannot enter,
> Ah! let us praise Diversity
> Which holds the world upon its center.[3]

Value has already been given to everything in creation by God's birthing it into being. Its value is its given function within a niche in the interconnecting webs of ecosystems, species, organs, tissues, cells, molecules and subatomic particles. Our present ethical and legal systems, which only give value to humans and to what humans value, are so hopelessly anthropocentric that they deserve a place in Garrett Hardin's suggested Museum of Obsolescence along with the notion of "an away you can throw things to."

Christopher Stone's proposal of rights for natural objects is a first step in an appropriate correction of such systems. If we truly honored the diversity in creation, we would move our culture to *a creation-based valuing of all the parts of nature.* We would not place the value of any one species always above the others. All species would be validated by their basic imprimatur of worth given to them in creation itself.

But some say to me: How could we possibly make decisions outside in the real world without valuing humans more than mosquitoes? How could we decide what to do, if all were of equal worth? My answer comes out of my experience with a similar situation in family life. Do parents consider all of their children to be of equal worth because they brought each of them into life? Then, if their children are of equal worth, how do parents make decisions about or between children? If the eldest is not superior because older or bigger, does the whole process of parental decision-making grind to a halt? Hardly! The point is that we parents continually find some grounds for making our decisions, grounds other than ranking our children in some hierarchy of their worth. What we perceive instead is that our children have differing needs, differing strengths, differing weaknesses. And occasions differ too. It is upon the basis of some convergence of all these factors that we make our decisions. And our decisions are always made within the overriding imperative that we seek to preserve the welfare of each of them as well as the welfare of the entire family!

It will be a new experience for humans to make decisions within creation's family *without* our confident assumption that "we are of course always the most loved and most valued child in creation's family." We will need to learn and gain practice in a different sort of decision-making. It will be, I think, a decision-making akin to the decision-making of parents. Such decision-making will appreciate diversity and reward it—without ranking it. Such decision-making finds value in each part as well as in the welfare of the whole. To say that such decision-making cannot be done outside the family in the "real world" is simply to prefer the thought-ways of the present because they are more familiar and therefore seem easier.

Consider these reflections upon the value of some other parts of creation:

If you are in the mood to be enchanted, stop, look, and notice fireflies. If these tiny insects came but once a decade, we would be arranging festivals for them, writing articles, and having private viewing parties to appreciate properly their nightly dance. Yet here they are for weeks absolutely free, transforming meadows, fields, backyards and lawns. These mysterious little creatures that baffle scientists with their ability to produce cold light are one of nature's most enchanting productions. Sit on your terrace some clear, moonless evening with all electric lights out and watch the night around you come alive with the weaving of a thousand pricks of light. This tiny light is their guide to each other.[4]

*   *   *

For several weeks our light blue delphinium in the perennial bed near the roses has been in full bloom. . . . It had been the center of interest for the local hummingbirds who come several times a day to sip nectar. Now today one little creature appeared, darting and hovering first here and then there. . . . The tiny bird rose in the air, perhaps ten feet high and a little to one side of the perennial bed. Flying so fast I could hardly follow him with my eye, he described an arc whose central low point was the delphinium itself. Here he swung back and forth like a pendulum in a great semi-circle. He did this about ten times and then took off.

I was fascinated by his performance, and by the brief glimpse into one of the many other worlds that interpenetrate ours. When it was over I rushed to the bird book and found that this is what hummingbirds do. The lady is always somewhere near the lowest part of the arc—next time I must look for her. It's a kind of courting dance although it seems a little late for courting now.[5]

The rainbow as a symbol in our time seems to be dawning, suggesting the spectrum of diversity we now are beginning to acknowledge and honor in our culture. A ray of light broken open by a prism into the whole spread of primary colors seems an apt metaphor or parable pointing to a creation which likewise breaks forth into all the variegate beauty of interdependent diversity. The rainbow is like a banner or flag, waving as a symbol of diversity over the movements of ethnicity and difference, celebrating the dissolution of the norm and of monochromatic uniformity. Let's hear it for the chocolate brown of the good earth and dark skins! Hurrah for roseate tones of sunsets and Indian skins. Cheers for the yellows of sunlight and oriental skins. Here's to the blue-purple of skies and butterflies. Let's celebrate the green of trees and all of nature's "niggers," and let's storm the law courts till we acknowledge the intrinsic value of *all* in creation's rainbow.

Human Identity Was Born a Twin

We have most especially misunderstood the covenant in creation which has come to us in human sexuality. As I write this I am in my daughter's bedroom enjoying a breeze from the land side of the house on a very hot day, and I am looking at a poster of hers which has intrigued me. It shows two strikingly striped black-and-white zebras and has the enigmatic inscription: "Happiness was born a twin."

Just so, human identity was born a twin. But not an identical twin, a different twin—a pair, one male and one female. But somehow the male-born could not handle this fact of "difference." Apparently the inner need has been irresistible to perceive this difference in hierarchical terms of who's above whom, so that men as mythmakers and portrayers of their worlds have in millenia past never understood and mythed the true dimensions of this human twinship and difference.

Always Woman Has Been Mythed Upon

Never has woman spoken for herself or mythed the world out of her own psyche. "Out of the relics of thirty thousand years," writes Elizabeth Janeway, "there is no image of woman that we can point to and say: This was made by women alone, apart from the eyes or direction of men." She then goes on to consider the earliest evidence:

> Take the earliest images of all, the little "Venuses" of the Old Stone Age which have been found across Europe and Asia from the Atlantic littoral to Siberia. To name them Venuses is to imply that they are goddesses; and so they have been called by many an archeologist. But look at them with a human eye: they are not goddesses, they are fetishes, lucky pieces for a desperate man, hunter or hunted, starving or wounded, to thumb in time of need; a memory of Mum and Mum's protection and thus not a portrait of woman, but of man's need for her. . . .

Even when the Goddess appears, her image is that of the woman seen by man from outside. She is the Great Mother, feared and adored, both mediator with and representative of necessity. This is not a picture drawn by woman. No girl child would form such an identity for herself, for there is nothing of her inner personal experience in it.... The Mother Goddess is an image shaped by emotions projected onto women, reflecting the desires and needs of others. In that pattern of making, a woman cannot be allowed to feel or express her own emotions, nor to originate any act, for her purpose is not to create her own life, but to validate the experience of others. *Her* experience isn't and can't be part of the reckoning, for it would confuse it hopelessly. It simply doesn't count and so she is absent from history.[6]

Simone de Beauvoir has written powerfully of how women have been mythed or imaged as "other"—that which is not-male. Elizabeth Janeway writes equally powerfully about what having woman as "other" has meant both to women and men.

Woman-as-other provides a focus for many needs and yearnings: for tenderness, given and asked for; for maternal protection; for divine assurance; for support against forces of depersonalization; for evidence of the existence of self-sacrifice and loving-kindness. Women are thought of by men (and thus they are instructed to be) upholders and transmitters of high virtues and values. They are validators of emotions and interpreters of experience. To men, this seems a role of great dignity and nobility, an elevation. Why do women refuse the pedestal?

How very hard it is for women to make clear that to the extent that one's life is spent as only a terribly necessary aspect of someone else's life, one ceases to be a person in oneself. To accept that one is "other" rather than human is to deny one's identity *as* a human and feel one's own personality as obtrusive, clouding the mirror one is supposed to be.[7]

One Twin's Curious Psychic Blindness

Mything the world always from the male viewpoint has resulted in a curious psychic blindness. This can be discerned in phrases such as Freud's "the fact of female castration." As Elizabeth Janeway sardonically observes, "What kind of fact can that be? So far as I know, no woman in Western society has suffered even the trauma of circumcision."[8] Only from the male point of view is the female castrated. From her point of view he has outside equipment he may seem obsessively and neurotically preoccupied with! Freud's remark is in the same category with "the body is the hero" and "flesh-colored Band-Aids" (which match only Caucasian flesh). When you think about these phrases, the blindness they reveal staggers the mind.

The ultimate problem with this dominance of male mything and imaging of the world is not its oppression of women *or* its effects upon men in any given generation. The most fundamental problem is that it has allowed the psyche of male culture to become a worldwide monoculture, with all the vulnerability ecologists are familiar with in biological monocultures. Only what male culture perceives is perceived. What male culture does not perceive does not exist for that male culture. The boardrooms and the seats of power are occupied by males and occasional token females carefully preselected from among those trained to perceive just like men. So there is no one to cry out, "Look! The emperor has no clothes on!"

The Other Twin Is Awakening

What is now happening to that other human twin? What of woman, who through the ages has been mythed upon? She stands, as Elizabeth Janeway so aptly put it, "between myth and morning."

> It is consciousness, it is presence, it is woman wakened from a millenial slumber and looking around at a world in which, astonishingly, one might be at home: Galatea without Pygmalion, dreaming herself out of the stone by her own force of creation.[9]

"It will be a long time yet," writes Janeway, "before we understand all that means, for first we have a great deal to unlearn."[10] We must unlearn all the male generic language and linear styles of thought we were so carefully taught in masculine culture. But more subtle, we must unlearn all the projections of female otherness—passivity, sexual seductiveness, the need to please, the expectation that woman will find her fulfillment in living vicariously for others. It becomes like starting again as a person, being born anew.

I still remember vividly a morning in a theological library some years ago when I read for the first time Valerie Saiving Goldstein's essay, "The Human Situation: A Feminine View."[11] I suddenly realized with her help that all of the theologians whose views I had so assiduously studied and assimilated in theological school were *male*! Valerie Saiving Goldstein was suggesting the possibility that their naming (or description) of the basic human condition as "anxiety" was a naming done from their male point of view. Perhaps women, she was suggesting, would name it differently. It was as if I had been engaged in a long, long game of intellectual Monopoly and suddenly I had been told: "Go back to Go. Do not collect $200. You must begin all over again." This was not good news. "You must try to 'undo' all that centuries of male thinking has done to you. And then you must see from your own flesh and your own intuition and your own experience how you yourself would name the human condition." This book has been my pilgrimage to do just that.

The woman really *is* between myth and morning. The consciousness of the woman-twin is just awakening. What lies ahead is a new interplay of male and female perspectives which goes beyond old stereotypes, a mutuality and symbiosis in which both are truly autonomous. I do not think masculine and feminine will then be understood in terms of androgyny and Jungian categories— which seem to me to accept that "masculine" is innately rational and active, while "feminine" is innately intuitive and passive. I doubt also that masculine and feminine will be cast in Yin/Yang terms— which again confine the one to activity and the other to passivity. And talk of "complementarity" in these matters usually means using the female to add what the male feels he is lacking. All of these ways of thinking still confine woman, define her territory for her, locate her in a psychic space defined and named from the male perspective and experience. Who but woman knows what woman is, how she perceives herself and world—until she awakes, and out of her own experience of herself and her own autonomy she myths for herself her world awake? Who knows yet what can be for the world and for creation's human twins—until they see and myth the world together, and each is "subject" mutually and none is "other"?

Yearning to Be "at Home" in the Earth

I have been saying in this chapter, first, that there is a covenant in creation itself which we have never understood and so have not been faithful to; second, that we have most especially misunderstood the covenant in creation which has come to us in human sexuality—in human identity being born a twin. Now all of this misunderstanding and misappropriation of creation has resulted in our alienation from each other and from the earth, our home. This alienation has been expressed in how we have thought and mythed God, ourselves, our world.

"If you put God outside," Gregory Bateson warns, "and set him vis-a-vis his creation and if you have the idea that you are created in his image, you will logically and naturally see yourself as outside and against the things around you. And as you arrogate all mind to yourself, you will see the world around you as mindless and therefore not entitled to moral or ethical consideration. The environment will seem to be yours to exploit. Your survival unit will be you and your folks or conspecifics against the environment of other social units, other races, and the brutes and vegetables."[12]

To myth ourselves apart is to myth ourselves alienated. Yet we yearn to be "at home"—at home with ourselves, at home with one another, at home with our world and our shared destinies that lead us through joys and pains and finally to our dying. In her quiet yet translucent description of her life in her home in New Hampshire May Sarton gives us a glimpse of an "at-homeness" in which the house, the woods, the meadows, the furniture from her past, the presences of friends and relatives mediated by flowers, habits, memories, and finally the silence, are all appropriate and interwoven into a wholeness of space and time.

> Silence was the food I was after, silence and the country itself—trees, meadows, hills, the open sky. I had wanted air, light, and space, and now I saw that they were exactly what the house had to give. The light here is magic. Even after all these years, it still takes me by surprise, for it changes with every hour of the day and with every season. In those first days it was a perpetual revelation, as sunlight touched a bunch of flowers or a piece of furniture and then moved on. Early in the morning I watched it bring alive the bronzed-gray of the bird's-eye maple of mother's desk in my study and make the flowers in the wreaths suddenly glow. In the afternoon, when I lay down for an hour in the cosy room, I saw it dapple the white mantlepiece and flow in waves across the wall there. And when I went into the kitchen to make tea, there it was again, lying in long dazzling rectangles on the yellow floor. This flowing, changing light plays a constant silent fugue, but in those first days I had still to learn how different the music is as the seasons come and go.

*   *   *

> Winter is the season when both animals and humans get stripped down to the marrow, but many animals hibernate, take the winter easy as it were; we humans are exposed naked to the currents of elation and depression. Here at Nelson it is the time of the most extraordinary light and the most perfect silence. When the first snow floats down on the rock-hard earth, first a flake at a time, then finally in soft white curtains, an entirely new silence falls. It feels as if one were being wound up into a cocoon, sealed in. There will be no

escape, the primitive person senses, always with the same shiver of apprehension. At the same time, there is elation. One is lifted up in a cloud, a little above the earth, for soon there is no earth to be seen, only whiteness—whiteness without a shadow, while the snow falls. Is it dawn or dusk? Who can tell? And this goes on all night and occasionally all the next day, until there is no way out of the house. I am sealed in tight. Many times during the night I wake to listen, listen, but there is no sound at all. The silence is as thick and soft as wool. Will the snow ever stop falling?

But when at last the sun comes out again, we are born into a pristine world, into the snow light. The house has become a ship riding long white slopes of waves. The light! It is like living in a diamond in this house where the white walls reflect the snow outside. There are shadows again, but now they are the most brilliant blue, lavender, even purple at dusk. And sooner or later I must push hard to open the front door against the drifts and get myself out with seed for the bird feeders. Then, when I come back to sit at my desk, I look out on an air full of wings as they come to dart, swoop, and settle—jays, nuthatches, chickadees, evening grosbeaks, woodpeckers, making a flurry of brilliant color across the white. The plows go roaring down the road, and I am safe inside with a fire burning in the study, lifted up on such excitement at my changed world that I can hardly sit still.[13]

The house itself, well-formed and graceful in design, spare and white, ordered and quiet. It seems a part of the woods and encroaching rough fields as birds and visiting animals and neighbors counterpoint May Sarton's solitude.

I found out very soon that the house demanded certain things of me. Because the very shape of the windows has such good proportions, because the builder cared about form, because of all I brought with me, the house demands that everywhere the eye falls it fall on order and beauty. So, for instance, I discovered in the first days that it would be necessary to keep the kitchen counter free of dirty dishes, and that means washing up after each meal; that the big room is so glorious, and anyone in the house is so apt to go to the kitchen windows to look out at the garden or into the sunset, that it would be a shame to leave it cluttered up. The white walls are a marvelous background for flowers, and from the beginning I have considered flowers a necessity, quite as necessary as food.

*   *   *

Choosing, defining, creating harmony, bringing that clarity and shape that is rest and light out of disorder and confusion—the work that I do at my desk is not unlike arranging flowers. Only it is much harder to get started on writing something!... Here again the house itself helps. From where I sit at my desk I look through the front hall, with just a glimpse of staircase and white newel post, and through the warm colors of an Oriental rug on the floor of the cosy room, to the long window at the end that frames distant trees and sky from under the porch roof where I have hung a feeder for woodpeckers and nuthatches. This sequence pleases my eye and draws it out in a kind of geometric progression to open space. Indeed, it is just the way rooms open into each other that is one of the charms of the house, a seduction that can only be felt when one is alone here. People often imagine that I must be lonely. How can I explain? I want to say, "Oh no! You see the house is with me." And it is with me in this particular way, as both a demand and a support, only when I am alone here.[14]

This is a portrait by one woman of her establishment of "at-homeness" within and around her. I don't think it is a making and mything of one's world and home you would expect of a man, even a man who was a writer. There is here a sturdy concreteness of attention to the form of living as well as a delicate sensitivity to the nuance of presence and to the past of memory. There is a pulling together of things cerebral and things physical, an interplay of the bounty of nature with the best subtleties of civilization. There is an openness to all that light and color, sound and texture, can bring—to all that human and animal, living and dead, surround one with.

Here the dead are not so much presences as part of the very fabric of my life; they are a living part of the whole. This way of absorbing death is not mourning. It does not look back romantically on the past; it builds the past into the present.So in a way I do not so much think about my father and mother as find myself in a hundred ways doing things as they would do. My mother tasted color as if it were food, and when I get that shiver of delight at a band of sun on the yellow floor in the big room, or put an olive-green pillow onto a dark-emerald corduroy couch, I am not so much thinking of her as being as she was.[15]

The Perverse Power of Negating Symbols

May Sarton indicates in her title "Plant Dreaming Deep" the role of dreaming, the role of mything, the role and power of *positive* symbolization. "I had first to dream the house alive inside myself," she writes.[16] But as we ourselves reach to create such at-homeness, the Genesis myth of the Fall intrudes upon the consciousness even of those who do not normally think of themselves as in any sense believers.

The powerful mythic tradition of which we are the involuntary inheritors has it that the harmonious life of the Garden of Eden existed only in some never-never land. We remain somehow deeply convinced that the lion will never lie down with the lamb, at least until some distant and unexpected Messiah comes. In short, to aspire to "being at home" with one's world, one's neighbors, one's self, is to evoke (from oneself as well as from others) the quashing epithet of Utopian or Romantic or hopelessly idealistic.

Through the centuries the doctrine of the Fall and its concommitant, the doctrine of Original Sin, have functioned to pronounce the very worst side of the human self as eternal and inescapable, at least in this life. It is not just that Adam and Eve in the myth were banished from the Garden. The doctrine of Original Sin (based upon that biblical myth) has come to have sufficient mythic power and universality to overwhelm and seem to negate our faltering human outreach toward any world of greater peace, justice and wholeness with the earth. The perverse power of this negating symbol has been to take all those goals which would otherwise be socially catalyzing and banish them to an Eden so irrelevant to our present lives and aspirations that it might just as well never have been. Eden has been portrayed as an unachievable Utopia we spoiled long ago and that we cannot now dream of or hope for or work toward, let alone live in—all because of the Fall.

The Genesis myth of the expulsion from the garden of Eden has been interpreted in the Christian tradition as "the Fall," even though the word "down" is not in the biblical account and there exists in Hebrew no word for "original sin." Jewish biblical scholars see no textual basis for what the Christian tradition has done with that bit of biblical material. Biblical theologian Bruce Birch has commented to me in private conversation that "Never have we hung such a large doctrine on such a slender strand of biblical material." Nonetheless, the Genesis account of the expulsion of Adam and Eve from the garden of Eden has been construed by the Christian tradition as the basis for the doctrine of the Fall and the sinfulness of Man. Both have functioned to legitimate as inevitable our worst side, to justify as normal "man's inhumanity to man," and to declare every non-oppressive social vision to be an impossible and sentimental dream.

A Vision of the Garden Revisited

We must re-myth our world! Lewis Mumford has observed that humanity dreams itself into existence.[17] Our old dream has become a nightmare; we must dream a better dream. Perhaps like the old woman I wrote of in chapter 6, we will see a new vision, a vision of the Garden revisited, without the old oppressive patriarchal stories. It is a vision of justice among groups, races, sexes, species. It is a vision of harmony, of wholeness. It is a vision of diversity and interconnection. It is a vision of human life—from the cell to the household to the whole human society—caught up in a symbiotic dance of cosmic energy and sensual beauty, throbbed by a rhythm that is greater than our own, which births us into being and decays us into dying, yet whose gifts of life are incredibly good though mortal and fleeting.

Perhaps what we need to do is to turn the Genesis myth upon its head. Perhaps this finite planet and the here-and-now *is* our Eden. Perhaps our forebears erred in thinking that we were expelled from Eden long ago in some pre-history we never knew. What if the Fall was not down into sin and our worst self but more ironically a Fall *up*—a Fall *up* in which we fail to accept or "claim" our full humanness, and the finitude of our bodies, and our mortality, and our trajectory toward dying? What if our Fall was *up* into the illusion that we were above dying, above mortality, above and apart from Creation?

Perhaps the limits of our finite planet are like the biblical angel with the flaming sword, ready to cast into outer darkness those unable to perceive and live within the mixed blessings of the creation that God has prepared equally for all species, all sexes, all races, all classes. Perhaps our appropriate aspiration is not "dominion" but "praise"!

*   *   *

> *This is the day which the Lord hath made,*
> Shining like Eden absolved of sin,
> Three parts glitter to one part shade:
> *Let us be glad and rejoice therein.*
>
> Everything's scoured brighter than metal.
> Everything sparkles as pure as glass—
> The leaf on the poplar, the zinnia's petal,
> The wing of the bird, and the blade of the grass.
>
> All, all is luster. The glossy harbor
> Dazzles the gulls that, gleaming, fly.
> Glimmers the wasp on the grape in the arbor.
> Glisten the clouds in the polished sky.
>
> Tonight—tomorrow—the leaf will fade,
> The waters tarnish, the dark begin.
> But *this is the day which the Lord hath made:*
> *Let us be glad and rejoice therein.*[18]

Notes

Chapter 1. Man-Above: The Anthropocentric Illusion

1. Walter Lippmann, *Public Opinion* (New York: Macmillan Co., 1922).
2. Lynn White, Jr., "The Historical Roots of Our Ecologic Crisis," *Science* 155 (1967): 1206.
3. Mary Daly, *Beyond God the Father: Toward a Philosophy of Women's Liberation* (Boston: Beacon Press, 1973), p. 3.
4. Judges 19:24.
5. Genesis 19:4-11.
6. Genesis 22.
7. Christopher D. Stone, writing in *Should Trees Have Standing?—Toward Legal Rights for Natural Objects* (Los Altos, Calif.: William Kaufmann, Inc, 1974), observes about the history of law that "even within the family, persons we presently regard as the natural holders of at least some rights had none. Take, for example, children. We know something of the early rights-status of children from the widespread practice of infanticide—especially of the deformed and female.... Maine tells us (in H. Maine, *Ancient Law* 153 (Pollock ed. 1930) that as late as the Patria Potestas of the Romans, the father had *jus vitae necisque*—the power of life and death—over his children. A fortiori, Maine writes, he had power of 'uncontrolled corporal chastisement; he can modify their personal condition at pleasure; he can give a wife to his son; he can give his daughter in marriage; he can divorce his children of either sex; he can transfer them to another family by adoption; and he can sell them.' The child was less than a person: an object, a thing." pp. 3-4.
8. William Irwin Thompson, *At the Edge of History: Speculations on the Transformation of Culture* (New York, Harper & Row, Harper Colophon Books, 1971), p. 69.
9. Thompson, *At the Edge of History,* p. 70.
10. Ida Hoos, "The Credibility Issue" and "Assessment of Methodologies for Radioactive Waste Management" in *Essays on Issues Relevant to the Regulation of Radioactive Waste Management, NUREG-0412* (Washington, D.C.: Office of Nuclear Material Safety and Safeguards, U.S. Nuclear Regulatory Commission, May 1978), pp. 20-30 and pp. 31-46. See also "The Trouble with Experts" in *Energy and the New Poverty,* by Katherine Seelman with David Dodson Gray (New York: Energy Education Project, Division of Church and Society, National Council of Churches of Christ, 1979), pp. 13-17.

Chapter 2. Does Human Uniqueness Mean Superiority?

1. Lisa F. Gray, "Revelations on a Glorious Day" (unpublished essay, November 15, 1975).
2. Peter Morgane, "The Whale Brain: The Anatomical Basis of Intelligence," in *Mind in the Waters: A Book to Celebrate the Consciousness of Whales and Dolphins,* ed. Joan McIntyre (New York: Charles Scribner's Sons/Sierra Club Books, 1974), pp. 85-86.
3. Morgane, p. 88.
4. Myron Jacobs, "The Whale Brain: Input and Behavior," in *Mind in the Waters,* p. 80.
5. Morgane, p. 93.
6. Carl Sagan, *The Cosmic Connection* (New York: Doubleday & Co., 1973), reprinted in *Mind in the Waters,* p. 88.
7. Paul Spong, "The Whale Show," in *Mind in the Waters,* p. 177.
8. Joan McIntyre, "Mind in the Waters," in *Mind in the Waters,* p. 220.
9. John Sutphen, "Body State Communication among Cetaceans," in *Mind in the Waters,* p. 141.
10. Sutphen, p. 142.
11. Research of Winthrop Kellogg cited in *Mind in the Waters,* p. 138.
12. Joan McIntyre, "On Awareness," in *Mind in the Waters,* p. 70.
13. Malcolm Brenner, "Say 'Rooo-beee!'" in *Mind in the Waters,* pp. 188, 189.
14. Joan McIntyre, *Mind in the Waters,* p.8.
15. John Lilly, "A Feeling of Weirdness," in *Mind in the Waters,* pp. 71-72.
16. Joan McIntyre, "Re-Creation," in *Mind in the Waters,* p. 237.

17. Carl Sagan, *The Dragons of Eden: Speculations on the Evolution of Human Intelligence* (New York: Random House, 1977), pp. 110–112.
18. Carl Sagan, *The Dragons of Eden*, p. 112.
19. Carl Sagan, *The Dragons of Eden*, p. 107.

Chapter 3. Psycho-Sexual Roots of Our Ecological Crisis

1. Ernest Becker, *The Denial of Death* (New York: Free Press, 1973), pp. 25–27.
2. Becker, p. 31.
3. Becker, pp. 50–51.
4. Rosemary Ruether, "Sexism and Liberation: The Historical Experience," in *From Machismo to Mutuality: Essays on Sexism and Woman-Man Liberation,* by Eugene C. Bianchi and Rosemary Radford Ruether (New York: Paulist Press, 1976), p. 15.
5. Ruether, pp. 15–16.
6. Becker, p. 162.
7. Becker, pp. 118–119.
8. Becker, pp. 39–40.

Chapter 4. From Nature-as-Mother to Nature-as-Wife

1. Charles W. Ferguson, *The Male Attitude: What Makes American Men Think and Act as They Do* (Boston: Little, Brown & Co., 1966), p. 227.
2. Ferguson, p. 234.
3. Ferguson, p. 17.
4. Ferguson, p. 17.
5. Ferguson, p. 274.
6. Fontaine Maury Belford, (untitled paper delivered as an address at Salem (North Carolina) State College, February 17, 1976, pp. 7–8.
7. Michelle Zimbalist Rosaldo, "Woman, Culture and Society: A Theoretical Overview," in *Woman, Culture and Society,* ed. Michelle Zimbalist Rosaldo and Louise Lamphere (Stanford, Calif.: Stanford University Press, 1974), p. 23.
8. Rosaldo, p. 24.
9. Sherry B. Ortner, "Is Female to Male as Nature Is to Culture?" in *Woman, Culture and Society,* p. 72.
10. *The Vocation of Man,* in *Johann Gottlieb Fichte's Popular Works,* compiled by W. Smith (London, 1873), p. 331. Cited by John Passmore, *Man's Responsibility for Nature: Ecological Problems and Western Traditions* (New York: Charles Scribner's Sons, 1974), p. 34.
11. W. A. Gauld, *Man, Nature and Time* (London, 1946), p. 124. Cited by Passmore, p. 35.
12. Edward Malins, *English Landscaping and Literature 1660–1840* (London, 1966), p. 99. Cited by Passmore, p. 36.
13. George Perkins Marsh, *Man and Nature* (New York, 1864), p. 43. Cited by Passmore, pp. 23–24.
14. Passmore, pp. 18–19.
15. Passmore, p. 5.
16. Margaret Mead, *Male and Female* (New York: William Morrow & Co., 1949).
17. H. R. Hays, *The Dangerous Sex: The Myth of Feminine Evil* (New York: G. P. Putnam's Sons, 1964).
18. Dorothy Dinnerstein, *The Mermaid and the Minotaur: Sexual Arrangements and Human Malaise* (New York: Harper & Row, 1976), p. 105.
19. Dinnerstein, p. 108.
20. Dinnerstein, pp. 109–110.
21. Dinnerstein, p. 104.
22. William Irwin Thompson, *At the Edge of History: Speculations on the Transformation of Culture* (New York, Harper & Row, Harper Colophon Books, 1971), p. 59.
23. Belford, p. 10.
24. Nancy Chodorow, "Family Structure and Feminine Personality," in *Woman, Culture and Society,* p. 46.
25. Lillian Smith, *Killers of the Dream* (1949; revised and enlarged ed., New York: Doubleday & Co., Anchor Books, 1961), pp. 113–116.
26. Chodorow, p. 50.

27. Warren Farrell, quoted in Barbara J. Katz, "A Quiet March for Liberation Begins," in *Men and Masculinity,* ed. Joseph H. Pleck and Jack Sawyer (Englewood Cliffs, N.J.: Prentice-Hall, Spectrum Books, 1974), p. 156.

28. Marc Feigen Fasteau, *The Male Machine* (New York: McGraw-Hill Book Co., 1974), pp. 14–15. The statements by executives are reported by Fernando Bartolome, "Executives as Human Beings," *Harvard Business Review* 50 (November-December, 1972): 65, 64.

29. David Halberstam, *The Best and the Brightest* (New York: Random House, 1972), pp. 531–532, cited by Fasteau, p. 173.

30. Fasteau, p. 176.

31. Eugene C. Bianchi, "Psychic Celibacy and the Quest for Mutuality," in *From Machismo to Mutuality* by Bianchi and Ruether, p. 88.

32. Glenn R. Bucher, ed., *Straight/ White/ Male* (Philadelphia, Penna.: Fortress Press, 1976).

33. Joseph H. Pleck and Jack Sawyer, ed., *Men and Masculinity* (Englewood Cliffs, N.J.: Prentice-Hall, Inc., Spectrum Books, 1974).

34. Eugene C. Bianchi, "The Super-Bowl Culture of Male Violence," in *From Machismo to Mutuality,* by Bianchi and Ruether, pp. 59–60.

35. Bianchi, p. 61.

36. Bianchi, pp. 62–63.

37. Quoted in Boston University *News,* March 14, 1974.

38. Dinnerstein, p. 242.

39. Dinnerstein, p. 169.

40. Chodorow, p. 50.

41. Rosaldo, pp. 40–41.

Chapter 5. The Threat of Death and the Appeal of Mastery.

1. Ian L. McHarg, *Design with Nature* (Garden City, N.Y.: Doubleday & Co., Doubleday/Natural History Press, 1971), p. 7.

2. Carl Sagan, *The Dragons of Eden: Speculations on the Evolution of Human Intelligence* (New York: Random House, 1977), pp. 52–54.

3. Charles W. Ferguson, *The Male Attitude: What Makes American Men Think and Act as They Do* (Boston: Little, Brown & Co., 1966), p. 172.

4. Langdon Winner, *Autonomous Technology: Technics-out-of-Control as a Theme in Political Thought* (Cambridge, Mass.: MIT Press, 1977), p. 20; p. 21; p. 23.

5. Karen Horney, *Neurosis and Human Growth: The Struggle toward Self-Realization* (New York: W. W. Norton & Co., Norton Library, 1950), p. 189; pp. 191–192.

6. Robert L. Harkel, *The Picture Book of Sexual Love* (New York: Cybertype Corp., 1973), p. 74.

7. Marc Feigen Fasteau, *The Male Machine* (New York: McGraw-Hill Book Co., 1974), p. 162.

8. Ernest Becker, *The Denial of Death* (New York: Free Press, 1973), pp. 3–4.

9. Becker, p. 5.

10. Bruno Bettelheim, *Symbolic Wounds: Puberty Rites and the Envious Male* (1954; new, revised edition, New York: Macmillan Co., Collier Books, 1962), p. 53; p. 30; p. 10.

11. David Riesman, (Book Review of *Symbolic Wounds*), *Psychiatry* 17 (1954): 300ff. Cited in Bettelheim, p. 11.

12. Karen Horney, *Feminine Psychology: Previously Uncollected Essays,* ed. Harold Kelman (New York: W. W. Norton Co., Norton Library, 1967), p. 115. See also pp. 134–146, pp. 106–118. "Men have never tired of fashioning expressions for the violent force by which man feels himself drawn to the woman, and side by side with his longing, the dread that through her he might die or be undone" (p. 134). "Is it not really remarkable (we ask ourselves in amazement), when one considers the overwhelming mass of this transparent material, that so little recognition and attention are paid to the fact of men's secret dread of women?... The man on his side has in the first place very obvious strategic reasons for keeping his dread quiet. But he also tries by every means to deny it even to himself. This is the purpose of the efforts to which we have alluded, to 'objectify' it in artistic and scientific creative work. We may conjecture that even his glorification of woman has its source not only in his cravings for love, but also in his desire to conceal his dread" (p. 136).

13. Charles W. Ferguson, *The Male Attitude: What Makes American Men Think and Act as They Do* (Boston: Little, Brown & Co., 1966), pp. 277–278.

14. Mircea Eliade, *From Primitives to Zen: A Thematic Source Book of the History of Religions* (New York: Harper & Row, 1974), Part 1, *Gods, Goddesses, and Myths of Creation,* p. 144.

Chapter 6. Turning to Another Way

1. Nancy Wood, *Many Winters: Prose and Poetry of the Pueblos* (Garden City, N.Y.: Doubleday & Co., 1974), p. 31.
2. Wood, p. 21.

Chapter 7. Discovering the Connections within the Structure of Reality

1. Jean Hersey, *The Shape of a Year* (New York: Charles Scribner's Sons, 1967), p. 149.
2. Ronald J. Glasser, *The Body Is the Hero* (New York: Random House, 1976), p. 207.
3. Glasser, pp. 18–19.
4. Glasser, p. 146.
5. Penelope Washbourn, "Body/World: The Religious Dimensions of Sexuality," *Christianity and Crisis* 34 (December 9, 1974): 279.
6. Glasser, pp. 147–148 (order of paragraphs rearranged).
7. Fritjof Capra, *The Tao of Physics: An Exploration of the Parallels between Modern Physics and Eastern Mysticism* (Berkeley, Calif.: Shambhala Publications, 1975), p. 22.
8. Capra, p. 23.
9. Capra, pp. 66-67.
10. Capra, p. 68.
11. Capra, p. 68.
12. Capra, pp. 77–78.
13. Capra, p. 203.
14. Capra, p. 203.
15. Capra, p. 64.
16. Capra, pp. 27–28.
17. Bunny McBride, "Beyond Words," *Christian Science Monitor,* 18 January 1977.
18. Capra, p. 68.
19. Capra, pp. 68–69.

Chapter 8. Distracted by Conflict from Seeing Whole

1. Loren Eiseley, *Darwin's Century: Evolution and the Men Who Discovered It* (Garden City, N.Y.: Doubleday & Co., Anchor Books, 1958), p. 37.
2. Lewis Thomas, *The Lives of a Cell: Notes of a Biology Watcher* (New York: Viking Press, 1974), p. 126.
3. Thomas, p. 29.
4. Thomas, p. 126.
5. Gordon Harrison, "Ecology: The New Great Chain of Being," *Natural History* 77, no. 10:8. Cited in "A Biologist's View of Nature," by Francisco J. Ayala, in *A New Ethic for a New Earth*, ed. Glenn C. Stone (New York: Friendship Press, 1971), pp. 38-39.
6. Eleanor and Clifford West, *Ossabaw* (Ossabaw, Ga.: Ossabaw Island Project, 1973), p. 30.
7. Jean Hersey, *The Shape of a Year* (New York: Charles Scribner's Sons, 1967), p. 108.
8. Hazel Henderson, *Creating Alternative Futures: The End of Economics* (New York: Berkley Publishing Corp., A Berkley Windhover Book, 1978), p. 403.

Chapter 9. Lost Dimensions of Human Identity

1. "The Myths We Live By," *Manas* (26 January 1977), p. 7.
2. Penelope Washbourn, "Body/World: The Religious Dimensions of Sexuality," *Christianity and Crisis* 34 (9 December 1974): 279.
3. Ronald J. Glasser, *The Body Is the Hero* (New York: Random House, 1976), pp. 226-248.
4. Glasser, p. 247.
5. Rene Dubos, "A Theology of the Earth," in *Western Man and Environmental Ethics,* ed. Ian G. Barbour (Reading, Mass.: Addison-Wesley, 1973), p. 44.
6. Kenneth Cauthen, "Toward a Theology of the Body," xerox (Rochester, N.Y.: Colgate Rochester Divinity School, 1971), p. 2.
7. Allen Wheelis, *On Not Knowing How to Live* (New York: Harper & Row, Colophon Books, 1975), pp. 40–41.

8. Sioux Indian proverb.

9. Ian L. McHarg, *Design with Nature* (Garden City, N.Y.: Doubleday & Co., Doubleday/Natural History Press, 1971), p. 29.

10. Lin Root in *Ossabaw,* by Eleanor and Clifford West (Ossabaw, Ga.: Ossabaw Island Project, 1973), p. 37.

Chapter 10. A New View of the Body

1. Eugene C. Bianchi, "Psychic Celibacy and the Quest for Mutuality," in *From Machismo to Mutuality: Essays on Sexism and Woman-Man Liberation,* by Eugene C. Bianchi and Rosemary Radford Ruether (New York: Paulist Press, 1976), pp. 87–88.

2. Bianchi, pp. 88–99.

3. Rosemary Ruether, "The Personalizatin of Sexuality," in *From Machismo to Mutuality,* p. 73.

4. Herb Goldberg, quoted in *Modern People,* 3 July 1977. See also Herb Goldberg, *The Hazards of Being Male: Surviving the Myth of Masculine Privilege* (New York: Nash Publishing Co., 1976), pp. 57–70.

5. Ruether, p. 70. The reference is to "On the Universal Tendency to Debasement in the Sphere of Love," by Sigmund Freud.

6. Bianchi, p. 123.

7. Dorothy Dinnerstein, *The Mermaid and the Minotaur: Sexual Arrangements and Human Malaise* (New York: Harper & Row, 1976), p. 73.

8. Rosemary Ruether, "Sexism and the Liberation of Women," in *From Machismo to Mutuality,* pp. 103–104.

9. Goldberg, *The Hazards of Being Male,* p. 110.

10. Penelope Washbourn, "Body/World: The Religious Dimensions of Sexuality," *Christianity and Crisis* 34 (December 9, 1974): 279. The ellipsis points are in the original.

11. Elise Maclay, *Green Winter: Celebrations of Old Age* (New York: Reader's Digest Press, 1977), p. 102.

12. The Wind passage, though expressed in the third person, was written by my husband to describe an experience we have often talked about.

13. J. A. Wheeler, in *The Physicist's Conception of Nature,* ed. J. Mehra (Dordrecht, Holland: D. Reidel, 1973), p. 244. Cited in Fritjof Capra, *The Tao of Physics: An Exploration of the Parallels between Modern Physics and Eastern Mysticism* (Berkeley, Calif.: Shambhala Publications, 1975), p. 141.

14. Alexandra Johnson, "Epiphany of Rain," *Christian Science Monitor,* 14 October 1976.

15. Ruether, p. 76.

16. Ruether, p. 71; p. 72.

Chapter 11. A Proper Sense of Death

1. Jean Hersey, *The Shape of a Year* (New York: Charles Scribner's Sons, 1967), p. 201.

2. Lewis Thomas, *The Lives of a Cell: Notes of a Biology Watcher* (New York: Viking Press, 1974), pp. 97-98; p. 98; pp. 98-99; p. 50; p. 50; p. 51.

3. Elisabeth Kuebler-Ross, *Death: The Final Stage of Growth* (Englewood Cliffs, N.J.: Prentice-Hall, Spectrum Books, 1975), p. 119, pp. 125–126.

4. Fontaine Belford, (unpublished speech), p. 15.

5. Charles W. Ferguson, *The Male Attitude: What Makes American Men Think and Act as They Do* (Boston: Little, Brown & Co., 1966), p. 280.

6. Ferguson, pp. 312–313.

7. William Stringfellow, *A Second Birthday* (Garden City, N.Y.: Doubleday & Co., 1970), p. 95; p. 95; p. 101; pp. 201–202.

8. Film produced by Francis Thompson, Inc., for Johnson Wax, *To Be Alive!* (New York: Macmillan Co., 1966), p. 18, p. 2.

9. Jean Hersey, *A Sense of Seasons* (New York: Dodd, Mead & Co., 1964), p. 40.

10. Huston Smith, *Forgotten Truth: The Primordial Tradition* (New York: Harper & Row, 1976), p. 143.

11. May Sarton, *Plant Dreaming Deep* (New York: W. W. Norton & Co., 1968), p. 125.

12. Bal Mount, M.D., "Letter to Elisabeth: Dedicated to Carol," in *Death: The Final Stage of Growth,* pp. 130-131.

13. Fritjof Capra, *The Tao of Physics: An Exploration of the Parallels between Modern Physics and Eastern Mysticism* (Berkeley, Calif.: Shambhala Publications, 1975), p. 244.
14. Jan Struther, *Mrs. Miniver* (New York: Harcourt, Brace & World, 1940), pp.3–4; pp. 5–6.
15. Elise Maclay, *Green Winter: Celebrations of Old Age* (New York: Reader's Digest Press, 1977), pp. 46–48.
16. Film, *To Be Alive!* end.
17. Struther, pp. 20–21.

Chapter 12. Woman as Bearer of a Different Consciousness

1. Jean Hersey, *A Sense of Seasons* (New York: Dodd, Mead & Co., 1964), p. 22.
2. Robert Jay Lifton and Eric Olson, *Living and Dying* (New York: Praeger, 1974), p. 30.
3. Lewis J. Perelman, "Elements of an Ecological Theory of Education" (Ph.D. diss., Harvard University, 1973), p. 134.
4. Audrey Drummond, "The Woman Infinite" xerox (Cambridge, Mass.: Harvard Divinity School, Theological Opportunities Program, 1977).
5. Penelope Washbourn, "Body/World: The Religious Dimensions of Sexuality," *Christianity and Crisis* 34 (December 9, 1974): 282–283.

Chapter 13. Moving with the Natural Grain of Life

1. "One Woman's Death—A Victory and a Triumph," by Dorothy Pitkin, ed. R. C. Townsend, in Elisabeth Kuebler-Ross, *Death: The Final Stage of Growth* (Englewood Cliffs, N.J.: Prentice-Hall, Spectrum Books, 1975), p. 107, 116, 116.
2. Ian L. McHarg, *Design with Nature* (Garden City, N.Y.: Doubleday & Co., Doubleday/Natural History Press, 1971), p. 11.
3. McHarg, p. 15.
4. McHarg, p. 9.
5. McHarg, p. 29.
6. Beatrice Willard, et al., "The Ethics of Biospheral Viability" in *Growth without Biospheral Disasters?* ed. Nicholas Polunin (London: Macmillan & Co., forthcoming).
7. Barry Commoner, *The Closing Circle: Nature, Man and Technology* (New York: Alfred Knopf, 1971), pp. 81–111.
8. Howard T. Odum, *Environment, Power and Society* (New York: Wiley-Interscience, 1971), pp. 274–303.
9. For an introduction to the New Alchemy Institute and its founder, John Todd, see *What Do We Use for Lifeboats When the Ship Goes Down?: Conversations with Robert Reines, John Todd, Ian McHarg, Paolo Soleri, and Richard Saul Wurman,* by "my" (New York: Harper and Row, Colophon Books, 1976), pp. 67–97.
10. my, pp. 77–79.
11. my, pp. 95–97.
12. Erik Eckholm and Lester R. Brown, *Spreading Deserts: The Hand of Man* (Washington, D.C.: World Watch Institute, 1977), pp. 29–30.
13. Matthias Johannessen, *Sculptor Asmundur Sveinsson: An Edda in Shapes and Symbols* (Reykjavik, Iceland: Iceland Review Books, 1974), p. 63.
14. Bianchi and Ruether, *From Machismo to Mutuality: Essays on Sexism and Woman-Man Liberation,* by Eugene C. Bianchi and Rosemary Radford Ruether (New York: Paulist Press, 1976), p. 61.
15. Jean Hersey, *The Shape of a Year* (New York: Charles Scribner's Sons, 1967), p. 137; p. 96; p. 104; p. 102.
16. May Sarton, *Plant Dreaming Deep* (New York: W. W. Norton & Co., 1968), p. 138.

Chapter 14. The Breaking Up of the Hierarchical Paradigm

1. Jean Hersey, *A Sense of Seasons* (New York: Dodd, Mead & Co., 1964), p. 164.
2. Kenneth Cauthen, "The Present and Future of Theology," in *Religion in Life* 45 (Autumn 1976): 314–315.
3. See for example Kenneth J. Arrow, *The Limits of Organization* (New York: W. W. Norton & Co., 1974) and Jay Galbraith, *Designing Complex Organizations* (Reading, Mass.: Addison-Wesley, 1973).
4. Elise Maclay, *Green Winter: Celebrations of Old Age* (New York: Reader's Digest Press, 1977), p. 112.

5. Frederick C. Thayer, *An End to Hierarchy! An End to Competition!: Organizing the Politics and Economics of Survival* (New York: Franklin Wats, New Viewpoints, 1973), p. 175.
6. Glenn R. Bucher, "The Oppressor Dehumanized," in *Straight/White/Male,* ed. Glenn R. Bucher (Philadelphia, Penna.: Fortress Press, 1976), p. 78.
7. Bucher, p. 79.
8. Bucher, p. 79.
9. Benjamin D. Berry, "Black Power and Straight White Males," in *Straight/White/Male,* p. 32. The quotation from Franz Fanon is from *Black Skin, White Masks,* trans. Charles L. Markmann (New York: Grove Press, 1967), p. 154.
10. Charles E. Lindner, "Maleness and Heterosexuality," in *Straight/White/Male,* p. 105.
11. Lindner, p. 102.
12. Dennis Altman, *Homosexual: Oppression and Liberation* (New York: Outerbridge and Lazard, 1971), p. 47. Cited in Bucher, p. 2.
13. Elizabeth Dodson Gray, "Television as Tribal Campfire," xerox (Cambridge, Mass.: MIT Sloan School of Management, Seminar 15.964, November 1975).
14. Cleveland Amory, *Man Kind?: Our Incredible War on Wildlife* (New York: Harper and Row, 1974).
15. Peter Singer, *Animal Liberation: A New Ethics for Our Treatment of Animals* (New York: New York Review/Random House, 1976).
16. Maurice K. Temerlin, review of *Animal Liberation, Psychology Today* 9, no. 10 (March 1976): 86.
17. Temerlin, p. 86.
18. Carl Sagan, *The Dragons of Eden: Speculations on the Evolution of Human Intelligence* (New York: Random House, 1977), p.121; pp. 120–121.
19. Seton Hall Law School, Newark, New Jersey.
20. Theodore S. Meth, "Should Some Animals Have Human Rights?," Boston *Globe* (24 July 1977), p. A-1.
21. David Ferleger, "The Battle over Children's Rights," *Psychology Today* 11, no. 2 (July 1977): 89.
22. Elizabeth Janeway, *Between Myth and Morning: Women Awakening* (New York: William Morrow & Co., 1975), pp. 185–214.
23. Aldo Leopold, *A Sand County Almanac with Essays on Conservation from Round River* (New York: Sierra Club/Ballentine Books, 1970), pp. 237–238.
24. Thomas Sieger Derr, *Ecology and Human Liberation: A Theological Critique of the Use and Abuse of Our Birthright* (Geneva, Switzerland: World Council of Churches, 1973), p. 46; p. 47, p. 47, p. 51, p. 53.
25. Derr, p. 35.
26. John Passmore, *Man's Responsibility for Nature: Ecological Problems and Western Traditions* (New York: Charles Scribner's Sons, 1974), p. 187.
27. Christopher D. Stone, "Should Trees Have Standing?: Toward Legal Rights for Natural Objects," 45 *Southern California Law Review* 450 (1972).
28. Christopher D. Stone, *Should Trees Have Standing?: Toward Legal Rights for Natural Objects* (Los Altos, Calif.: William Kaufmann, 1974), p. 11.
29. Stone, p. 5.
30. Stone, p. 24.
31. Stone, pp. 6–8.
32. Jean Hersey, *The Shape of a Year* (New York: Charles Scribner's Sons, 1967), p. 163.
33. The Findhorn Community, *The Findhorn Garden: Pioneering a New Vision of Man and Nature in Cooperation* (New York: Harper and Row, Colophon Books, 1975).
34. Jean Hersey, *A Sense of Seasons* (New York: Dodd, Mead & Co., 1964), pp. 36–37; p. 37–38; p. 37.

Chapter 15. We Must Re-Myth Genesis

1. Archibald Rutledge, *Peace in the Heart* (Garden City, N.Y.: Doubleday & Co., 1927). Cited in *These Times* (April 1977), p. 8; p. 9; p. 9; p. 11.
2. Rutledge, cited in *These Times,* p. 11.
3. Phyllis McGinley, "In Praise of Diversity," in *The Love Letters of Phyllis McGinley* (New York: Viking Press, Compass Books, 1954), pp. 12–14, selections.
4. Jean Hersey, *A Sense of Seasons* (New York: Dodd, Mead & Co., 1964), p. 170.

5. Jean Hersey, *The Shape of a Year* (New York: Charles Scribner's Sons, 1967), pp. 135–136.
6. Elizabeth Janeway, *Between Myth and Morning: Women Awakening* (New York: William Morrow & Co., 1975), pp. 3–4.
7. Janeway, pp. 206–207.
8. Janeway, p. 150.
9. Janeway, pp. 2–3.
10. Janeway, p. 7.
11. Valerie Saiving Goldstein, "The Human Situation: A Feminine Viewpoint," in *The Nature of Man,* ed. Simon Doniger (New York: Harper and Bros., 1962).
12. Gregory Bateson, *Steps to an Ecology of Mind* (New York: Ballentine Books, 1972), p. 462.
13. May Sarton, *Plant Dreaming Deep* (New York: W. W. Norton & Co., 1968), p. 55; pp. 85–86.
14. Sarton, p. 57; pp. 57–59.
15. Sarton, p. 184.
16. Sarton, p. 31
17. Lewis Mumford, "Reflections," *New Yorker,* 1975. Cited by Dorothy Dinnerstein, *The Mermaid and the Minotaur: Sexual Arrangements and Human Malaise* (New York: Harper & Row, 1976), p. 251.
18. Phyllis McGinley, "Sunday Psalm," in *Love Letters,* p. 32. Emphasis added.

13 5 - 6